THE "SECRET" GOSPEL OF MARK:

Morton Smith, Clement of Alexandria, and Four Decades of Academic Burlesque.

ROBERT CONNER

Copyright © 2015 Mandrake & Robert Conner

All rights reserved. No part of this work may be reproduced or utilized in any form by any means electronic or mechanical, including *xerography*, *photocopying*, *microfilm*, and *recording*, or by any information storage system without permission in writing from the publishers.

Also by Robert Conner
Jesus The Sorcerer: Exorcist, Prophet of The Apocalypse
Magic in The New Testament: a survey and appraisal of the evidence
Magic in Christianity: From Jesus to Gnosticism (see page 158 below)

Published by
Mandrake of Oxford
PO Box 250
OXFORD
OX1 1AP (UK)

A CIP catalogue record for this book is available from the British Library and the US Library of Congress.

Cover art by Christopher Cochran

CONTENTS

PREFACE, 5-8.

MAR SABA, 1958, 9-22.

THE LETTER TO THEODORE, 23-37.

SMITH'S INTERPRETATION, 38-52.

THE ACADEMY RESPONDS, 53-74.

ATTACK OF THE ULTRACREPIDARIANS, 75-115.

THE BELOVED DISCIPLE, 116-141.

LEFT BEHIND, 142-149.

REFERENCES, 150-157.

PREFACE

The discovery of missing verses belonging to the gospel of Mark, the earliest of the canonical gospels, would be riveting news indeed to those interested in the origins of Christianity. In 1973, Morton Smith, a history professor at Columbia University, claimed to have found verses from an early edition of Mark quoted in a letter from a church official, Clement of Alexandria, and published an account and analysis of his finding in two books, one scholarly, the other popular.[1] Today, over forty years later, the New Testament studies guild is divided over the authenticity of the find and scholars have accused Smith of forging both the Marcan material and the letter of Clement in which it appears.

Prior to 2006, I translated the Marcan verses—which according to Smith came from an edition of the gospel he called *Secret Mark*—as well as the letter attributed to Clement as part of a chapter in a book on magic in the career of Jesus.[2] If Smith's find proved to be authentic, the excision of the missing verses and their subsequent restoration would be *the* case study of the manipulation of the text of an early gospel. It could prove that the canonical gospel of Mark is an expurgated text from which some amount of potentially

---

[1] Smith, *Clement of Alexandria and a Secret Gospel of Mark*, 1973, Harvard University Press and *The Secret Gospel: The Discovery and Interpretation of the Secret Gospel According to Mark*, 1973, Harper & Row.

[2] Conner, *Jesus the Sorcerer: Exorcist and Prophet of the Apocalypse*, 2006, Mandrake of Oxford.

embarrassing material had been removed by the author or an editor of the gospel as early as the mid-1st century.

As time has passed and the debate over authenticity sputters on, the "Secret" gospel controversy has proven to be an outstanding example of a different process, the response of New Testament scholars to an unwelcome interpretation of the teaching of Jesus of Nazareth. I will argue that in their attempt to discredit Smith, some members of the Jesus Studies community have raised fatal questions about their own credibility, methodology and, frankly speaking, about their own credulity.

Like some others who accept the authenticity of the Clement letter, I questioned parts of Smith's interpretation of it almost from the beginning, particularly the claim that the letter refers to a baptismal initiation ritual. Smith believed that the linen cloth mentioned in the first of the "Secret" gospel fragments was a baptismal garment, but I saw no evidence then or now in the letter of Clement or in the canonical gospel of Mark for such a claim. On the other hand, inserting the fragments into the canonical gospel of Mark results in a smoother, more coherent narrative arc; the verses quoted by Clement fit back into the canonical gospel naturally, like the missing pieces of a puzzle, and like the missing pieces of a puzzle, the restored verses neatly resolve several stubborn aporia that have defied previous attempts to explain them. In any event, Smith chose to stick with his baptismal interpretation rather than following the story to a different, and in my view far more convincing, conclusion.

In subsequent books on magic in early Christianity I chose not to use the "Secret" Mark material. I replaced it with more direct evidence for magical praxis in the career of Jesus and the early Christians, evidence so abundant that I doubt a complete treatment of it would fit into less than a thousand pages. At the urging of my editor, the chapter on "Secret" Mark in *Jesus the Sorcerer* became an online essay and when it came time to update and refine the essay, my editor suggested it be turned into a short book, the work you are now reading.

The "Secret" Mark saga is complex, encumbered nearly from the start by specious claims, misinformation, silly arguments, and gay bashing. It is not my purpose to rehearse each and every zig and zag the controversy has taken over the past forty years—well beyond my patience and the reader's endurance—nor will I dwell on the hermeneutics of scandal or the recitation of charges demonstrated to lack merit except as necessary to illustrate questionable strategies and failed tactics of argumentation.

It is my hope that readers interested in the New Testament and early Christianity generally own at least some basic facility in Greek since the founding documents of Christianity and most of the early texts of interest are in Greek. The focus of this work will be on what relevant texts say and only secondarily on how specialists interpret the texts. That said, those whose linguistic reach in Greek exceeds their grasp should still be able to follow the string leading out of the labyrinth of the "Secret" Mark debate, a maze into which many have ventured and few returned.

I should emphasize that I have come to the issue from outside the academy and far removed from the circle of Christian belief. Like many who have followed the frenzy of this debate, usually with interest, often with amusement, but more often with dismay, I have concluded that whatever it may or may not reveal about the early gospels, it reveals important truths about New Testament scholars. As Smith so aptly observed, "…there is something strange about the documents, or about the scholars who have studied them, or both. Probably both. Most of the scholars have not been historians, but theologians determined to make the documents justify their own theological positions."[3] Whatever one makes of Smith's conclusions—which are certainly open to criticism—it is clear that he was spot on about the scholars.

[3.] Smith, *Jesus the Magician*, 3.

MAR SABA, 1958

Smith at Mar Saba, early 1980's.

Titus Flavius Clemens, known as Clement of Alexandria (died circa 215 CE), was almost certainly initiated into one or more of the mystery cults before converting to Christianity.[4] Clement attempted a synthesis of Christian theology with

---

4. "Christian writers converted from paganism may, of course, have been initiated in their youth and on this ground the evidence of Arnobius and Clemens is a priori superior..." Farnell, *The Cults of the Greek States*, II, 128.

pagan philosophy—the subject of his *Exhortation to the Greeks*—and revealed how easily Christian doctrine could be expounded in the language and imagery of the pagan mysteries, as well as how closely magic and mystery cults intertwined:

> Let us sweep away then, sweep away forgetfulness of the truth, the ignorance and the darkness, the obstacle that like *a mist* (αχλυς)[5] slips down over our sight. *Let us see a vision* (εποπτευσωμεν)[6] of what is really and truly divine, first of all singing out to Him this cry, *Welcome, Light* (Χαιρε Φως)! Light for us from heaven! For we who lie buried in darkness and have been wrapped up in the shadow of death!
>
> ...If, on the one hand, those who have trusted in the sorcerers receive *amulets and enchantments* (τα περιαπτα και τας επαοιδας) merely purported to bring deliverance, do you not rather resolve to put on the heavenly [amulet], the Word that saves, and *trusting in*

---

[5]. A *mist*, or if the reference is to Homer, the *film* that forms on the eyes of the dying (*Iliad* V, 696). Athene removes "the mist" (την αχλυν) that dulls men's eyes. (Philostratus, *The Life of Apollonius of Tyana*, VII, 32). The term had magical and theurgic connotations in Neoplatonic thought (Collins, *Magic in the Ancient World*, 128).

[6]. From εποπτευω, *to be admitted* into the highest grade of the mysteries, become an εποπτης (epoptēs), one who has achieved the final step of initiation and seen all that is to be revealed. The same terminology is used in 2 Peter 1:16.

the enchantment of God (τη επωδη του θεου πιστευσαντες) *be delivered from passions*...[7]

O the truly holy mysteries (Ω των αγιων ως αληθως μυστηριων)! *O pure light! Being enlightened* (δαδουχουμαι),[8] *I am initiated* (εποπτευσαι) *into the highest mysteries of the heavens and of God! I become holy by being initiated* (αγιος γινομαι μυουμενος)!

...*The Lord reveals the mysteries* (ιεροφανται δε ο κυριος)[9] *and places his seal upon the initiate when he has believed, and lighting his way, conducts him to the Father, where he is protected for all ages*...*These are my mysteries, my Bacchic revelries* (ταυτα των εμων μυστηριων τα βακχευματα).[10] *If you desire, be initiated yourself and you will dance with angels around* (χορευσεις μετ' αγγελων)[11] *the unbegotten and undying and only true God while the Word of God chants along with us* (συνυμνουντος ημιν).[12]

[7.] "In accord with theurgy's Platonizing tendencies, these demons were interpreted by the theurgists as the inflictors of corporeal passions that would lure the soul away from its proper pursuits..." (Johnston, *Restless Dead*, 137).

[8.] From δαδουχος (dadouchos), *torch bearer*, an official in the Eleusinian mysteries.

[9.] Jesus is the ιεροφαντης (hierophantēs), the *hierophant*, the revealer of the mysteries. The hierophant is an initiator who reveals what is holy as Clement's next words make clear.

[10.] The βακχευμα (bakcheuma), the frenzied nocturnal rites of Bacchus.

[11.] From χορευω (choreuō), *dancing in the round*, used of religious rites, particularly of the Bacchic chorus.

Clement ingenuously refers to the heavenly Christ as an *amulet* and salvation as an *enchantment,* describing his Christian faith in the terms and imagery of a riotous Dionysian celebration. The normally staid Clement casts himself as a χορευτης (choreutēs), or θιασωτης (thiasōtēs), an ecstatic follower of Christ, dancing madly in the throes of possession. His imagery of dancing with angels deliberately recalls ecstatic rites. MacMullen describes the difficulty the church faced in banning elements of ecstatic ritual from Christian assemblies: "Ambrose of Milan...witnessed his congregation dancing during times of worship. (He seems to mean right inside the churches, but he does not supply details.) He was shocked. Such conduct was pagan."[13] That Clement could speak of Christ in frankly magical terms reflected contemporary Christian thought. "An amulet intended to provide protection against illness and the power of evil" preserves this wording: "for the seal of Jesus Christ is written upon my forehead..."[14] During Clement's life it is probable that the Christian movement in Alexandria consisted of "a number of esoteric groups"[15] in which gnosis, divinely revealed knowledge, led step by step to perfection.

[12.] To chant a υμνος (humnos), *hymn* or *festal song*, in honor of the god along with the rest of the Bacchic throng. Clement, *The Exhortation to the Greeks*, XI, XII. I have used the Greek text of the Loeb edition (pages 242, 244-246, 256), but the translation is my own.

[13.] MacMullen, *Christianizing the Roman Empire*, 74.

[14.] Meyer, *Ancient Christian Magic*, 113, 115.

[15.] Klijn, *The Roots of Egyptian Christianity*, 173.

Although Clement, the head of the catechetical school in Alexandria, was no minor figure, during the 16th century his feast day, December 4th, was dropped from the calendar after his writings came to be viewed as doctrinally tainted, an event that reflected the tendency of the Catholic Counter-Reformation to distance itself from anything that emitted the slightest whiff of heresy or magic. As indicated by the brief excerpts given above, the forces of Catholic orthodoxy may have been on to something—comparing Christ to Bakchos, whose rites included "altered states such as trance, masquerade, madness, and of course, intoxication"[16] pushes the envelope a bit far. Clement clearly reflects an age in which the line between Christian teaching and mystery cult was fuzzy, at least so far as he was concerned. It is, however, richly ironic that Clement, one of the earliest Christian apologists, should be declared heretical by the very religion he sought to establish and defend.

In any case, Scott Brown's conclusion would seem to fit the evidence: "The Letter to Theodore therefore is intentionally employing imagery from the mystery religions to describe the function of the mystical gospel, specifically, imagery related to the highest grade of initiation, the great mysteries…The Letter to Theodore and the mystical gospel are examples of Christian esotericism, the attitude that the highest truths do not belong to everyone but are reserved for those who are capable of comprehending them."[17]

[16.] Larson, *Ancient Greek Cults*, 127.

[17.] Brown, *The Fourth* R 26/1, 7, 21.

The modern story of the letter of Clement begins with Morton Smith (1915-1991). A history professor at Columbia at the time of his discovery, Smith visited the monastery of Mar Saba previously in 1941 as a graduate student. Trapped in Palestine by the Second World War, he used the opportunity to study at the Hebrew University in Jerusalem and received a Ph.D. in 1948—his dissertation was written in Hebrew. He took a second Ph.D. in theology from Harvard University. Given these facts, it would be tempting to overestimate Smith's facility with Hebrew, but as Allan Pantuck reveals, it took Smith years to acquire proficiency in Hebrew and he found it necessary to read Hebrew text weekly with a rabbinical scholar to maintain his skill.[18]

In 1958 Smith revisited the monastery of Mar Saba, a Greek Orthodox hermitage located 12 miles southeast of Jerusalem in the Kidron Valley between the city and the Dead Sea. The monastery, founded about the year 484 and named after Saint Sabbas (439-532), is older than the more famous Saint Catherine's Monastery in the Sinai.

The purpose of Smith's visit in 1958 was a search for manuscript material in the monastery's two libraries. However, *libraries* in this case did not refer to manicured book stacks zealously maintained by a professional staff. The volumes of the Mar Saba libraries, which would likely have been housed in the special collections division of a university, were a "chaos of old books...books and manuscripts piled every which way on the floor and in bookcases."[19] In short, the condition of the books Smith encountered betrayed an

---

[18.] Pantuck, *Ancient Gospel or Modern Forgery?*, 185-191.

attitude of casual neglect as well as ignorance of and disregard for the value of ancient texts, and the fact that a monk accompanied Smith to the library and kept him under observation suggests that the real purpose of the library was to sequester books. Reading Smith's account I am reminded of Eco's character Malachi of Hildesheim in *The Name of the Rose*, a librarian whose primary, and perhaps only, duty is to obstruct access to books. In any case, it is clear that the monks at Mar Saba were not conservators of valuable texts; the pages of medieval manuscripts had been pasted together "to make cardboard for binding more recent works."[20] As we shall see, careless handling and indifference to the preservation of irreplaceable texts on the part of the Greek Orthodox Church continues to be a serious issue.

Toward the end of his visit at Mar Saba, Smith happened upon two and a half pages of writing in the end pages of a damaged copy of Voss' 1646 edition of the letters of Ignatius.[21] On closer examination the text appeared to be part of a previously unknown letter of Clement of Alexandria, perhaps copied from a surviving collection of Clement's correspondence. Excited by his discovery, Smith took photographs of the handwritten pages and at the end of his

---

[19] Smith, *The Secret Gospel*, 10. One may compare Smith's photo of the tower library (*The Secret Gospel*, 34) that shows a clutter of material in a state of disarray.

[20] Ibid, 11.

[21] Voss, *Epistolae genuinae S. Ignatii Martyris*. Charles Hedrick's "An Amazing Discovery," *Biblical Archaeology Review*, November / December, 2009, 44-48, contains a recent summary of the circumstances of Smith's find.

stay returned the volume to the shelf. His subsequent studies were done from his photographs. The book did not belong to Smith; removing it without permission would have been theft. At no point did Smith have any control over access to the Voss book or to the end pages containing the letter, nor did Smith attempt to impede access to the material.

Clement was a prolific writer, but no personal correspondence attributed to him is known to be extant, little surprise since the survival of correspondence appears to be quite rare. However, that some of his letters existed for centuries after his death appears certain—"a collection of Clement's letters existed at Mar Saba when John of Damascus, who worked there from 716 to 749, quoted three passages from the collection in his *Sacra Parallela* ..."[22] Of the apostolic fathers—to the best of my knowledge—no letters of Papias or Justin Martyr still exist. A single letter of Polycarp is known, two of Ireneus, and seven of Ignatius. Of the church fathers of the 2nd century, no letters of Tatian, Theophilus or Athenagoras are known to be extant.

The Clement letter contains items of intense interest: two exact quotations from a previously unknown edition of the gospel of Mark—which Smith called *Secret Mark*—and mention of an early heretical sect, the Carpocratians. By any reckoning, it was a significant discovery. Smith spent years carefully analyzing his findings and published the results in

---

[22.] Smith, *Clement of Alexandria*, 285. "Actually, John [of Damascus] quoted from three letters among which one was said to be letter number 21. So there were *at least* 21 letters." Roger Viklund, personal communication.

two venues, one scholarly, the other popular, in 1973. Smith had previously announced the existence of his discovery in 1960 at a meeting of the Society for Biblical Literature.

Clement of Alexandria and a Secret Gospel of Mark, published by Harvard University Press in 1973, is a 454-page collaborative work of detailed textual analysis. To determine the approximate date of the letter's composition, Smith enlisted the assistance of ten experts in paleography who placed the time of writing somewhere around 1750.[23] Sixteen noted biblical scholars affiliated with major American and European universities read the first draft of Smith's work on the text of the letter and their observations were incorporated into Smith's commentary. Smith specifically acknowledged Bickerman (Columbia), Calder (Columbia), Chadwick (Oxford), Einarson (Chicago), Früchtel (Ansbach), Grant (Chicago), Hadas (Columbia), Jæger (Harvard), Lampe (Cambridge), Mondésert (Lyon), Munck (Arhus), Nock (Harvard), Reumann (Lutheran Theological Seminary), Richard (Paris), Richardson (Union Theological Seminary), Schippers (Amsterdam), Völker (Mainz), Wifstrand (Lund), and "a number of other scholars who have commented on particular passages."[24]

[23.] Smith, *Clement of Alexandria*, 1.

[24.] Ibid, 6. "…he scrupulously acknowledges the comments of the large number of scholars from all over the world to whom he submitted, for their comments and reactions, various materials included within the book. The fact that many comments disagree with his own views and present alternative explanations has not dissuaded Smith from including them." (Achtemeier, *Journal of Biblical Literature* 93 (1974): 625).

The unavoidable impression upon reading Smith's work is that he took his discovery very seriously. His commentary includes extensive material on vocabulary and parallels with confirmed Clementine writings, as well as historical background, including details of Hellenistic magical practice, Christian splinter sects, and evidence for the probable existence of more philosophically advanced groups within early Christian centers—"*ecclesiola in ecclesia.*" [25] In *Clement of Alexandria*, Smith's impressive abilities as a linguist and historian are on full display. Stroumsa says of Smith's work that it "shows a philologist fully mastering his craft"[26] and Anthony Grafton remarked of Smith, an experienced manuscript hunter, "Though American by birth and most of his education, he was a great philologist in the old European style. Long before he made the Mar Saba discovery, he had mastered Latin, Greek and Hebrew, and examined and photographed Greek manuscripts in monastic libraries on Mount Athos, the island of Patmos and elsewhere."[27]

It is easy to suspect that some of Smith's most vocal detractors have never bothered to read *Clement of Alexandria*, and that in any case few of them are qualified to critique Smith's work in any meaningful way. At least one authority on the New Testament who has such qualifications has characterized *Clement of Alexandria* as "an amazing book of scholarship."[28]

[25.] Ibid, 283.
[26.] Stroumsa, *Morton Smith and Gershom Scholem*, xiv.
[27.] Grafton, *The Nation*, January 26, 2009, 25.
[28.] Ehrman, *Lost Christianities*, 76.

The popular version, *The Secret Gospel: The Discovery and Interpretation of the Secret Gospel According to Mark*, originally published by Harper & Row, was reissued by Dawn Horse Press in 1982, 1984, and 2005. Although Smith characterized his discovery as a "Secret Gospel," and the term has become entrenched in the literature, I prefer the term *Longer Mark*, following Scott Brown's insights in that regard.[29]

In response to *Clement of Alexandria*, a few writers expressed doubts that the discovery of a letter was even possible, but this appears to be a transparent reaction to its unwelcome contents, not to the probability of its preservation.[30] It is hardly incredible that a letter of Clement could have survived for centuries and that it might turn up in—of all places!—one of Christendom's most ancient monasteries, a hermitage in use for 1500 years, copied into a volume of the letters of Ignatius, another early church writer.

> "It is known that Clement of Alexandria wrote letters. But not one of these letters had survived, although quotations from Clement's letters appear in the *Sacra Parallela* attributed to John of Damascus who stayed at the Mar Saba Monastery from the beginning of the 8th century to his death (ca. 750 CE). The first question was, therefore, whether this letter was indeed the copy of a genuine letter of the Alexandrian Father. There are a number of scholars

---

[29.] Brown, *Mark's Other Gospel*, 121-135.

[30.] An invaluable summary of the reaction to Smith's claims has been written by Shawn Eyer (*Alexandria: The Journal for the Western Cosmological Traditions* 3 (1995): 103-129).

who have expressed doubts with respect to its authenticity. However, vocabulary, style, syntax, and manner of quotation in the letter are either identical with, or similar to, that of Clement's genuine writings. Skepticism is hard to justify."[31]

Smith spent over a decade in all studying the Clement letter, attempting to place it in the historical context of early Christianity. In the end, Smith concluded that an Aramaic original lay behind the canonical Greek gospel of Mark and that Mark had been "reworked at least four times—by the author of secret Mark, by Matthew, by Luke, and by the Carpocratians (who are said to have used secret Mark)."[32] Nevertheless, he clearly understood that conjecture about things not meant to be known, "to explain what ancient authors deliberately concealed,"[33] is risky at best.

My personal opinion, shared by a minority, is that *Longer* ("Secret") *Mark* was the original form of the gospel from which some unknown quantity of material was subtracted to produce canonical Mark, and like Smith, I believe that *Longer Mark* shared a source that is the basis for the story of Lazarus in the gospel of John, a hypothetical scenario defended later on in this book.

[31.] Koester, *Ancient Christian Gospels*, 293-294.
[32.] Smith, *The Secret Gospel*, 142.
[33.] Ibid, 143.

THE LETTER TO THEODORE

My translation of the letter to Theodore appears below (the citations from *Longer Mark* are italicized). Since Smith's opinions on his discovery have often been drowned out by controversy, not to mention hostile and dishonest interpretations, the reader is frequently referred back to *Clement of Alexandria* in the footnotes so that Smith's voice can be heard. The footnotes also seemed to be a convenient way to identify vocabulary items that have figured in the debate, record the remarks and opinions of commentators and to sketch the magico-religious background of the 2nd century.

> From the letters of the Most Holy Clement of the *Stromateis*:
>
> To Theodore:[34]
>
> You did well to silence *the unmentionable teachings* (τας αρρητους διδασκαλιας)[35] of the Carpocratians, for they

---

[34.] The identity of Theodore is unknown. Smith observed, "A reference to a famous recipient would have been much more suspicious. Who would have forged a letter to a nobody?" (*The Secret Gospel*, 25).

[35.] Clement uses αρρητος, *unspoken, not to be divulged*, "of the Eleusinian mysteries, emphasizing their sexual symbolism…" (Smith, *Clement*, 8).

are the wandering stars that were foretold. They stray from the narrow path of the commandments toward the bottomless pit of sins of the flesh embodied, for having been inflated with the *knowledge* (γνωσις)—as they call it—of the deep things of Satan, they fail to notice that they are plunging themselves into the outer darkness of falsehood, and while bragging about being free, they have become slaves of despicable cravings. Such men are always to be resisted in all ways, for even if they speak truthfully, even so, a lover of truth should not agree with them, for neither are all true things truth, nor should what appears to be true according to *human opinions* (ανθρωπινας δοξας)[36] take precedence over the true truth which is in accord with faith.[37]

Now concerning the things they keep chattering about regarding the divinely inspired Gospel according to Mark, some are complete lies, and others, even if they contain some truth, are not accurately represented, for the truth, having been mixed up with inventions, is

---

[36.] "Human opinions" is used by Clement "to describe the secret doctrines of the mystery cults. (As these are hidden from the ignorant, how much more should the holy science of Christianity be hidden!)" (*Clement*, 15).

[37.] "It is characteristic of Clement to talk most of truth when recommending falsity." (*Clement*, 14). Smith devoted some space to a discussion of "white lies," the practice of deception for a good purpose and "truth" technically and narrowly defined. (*Clement*, 53-54).

thereby falsified so that—as the saying goes—even the salt loses its flavor.

As for Mark, during Peter's stay in Rome, he wrote down the things the Lord did, *not, however, revealing everything* (ου μεντοι πασας εξαγγελλων),[38] much less hinting at *the mysteries* (τας μυστικας),[39] but selecting what he considered advantageous for increasing the faith *of those being instructed* (των κατηχουμενων).[40] When Peter suffered martyrdom, Mark came to Alexandria, preserving both his own *recollections* and

---

[38.] The verb εξαγγελω, *to betray a secret*, and εξαγγελος, *informer*. "It is used elsewhere in this sense concerning the mystery cults...," i.e., of those who revealed the secret contents of the mystery rites. (*Clement*, 24).

[39.] From μυστικος, *related to the mysteries, private, secret*, a predominantly pagan usage particularly of the rites of Bacchus —"the mystic [chant] Iacchus" (τον μυστικον ιακχον), (Herodotus 8.65). The New Testament writers favor μυστηριον, *mystery, secret rite* or *revelation*, also used of pagan ritual.
"Μυστηριον is part of Clement's esoteric vocabulary, marking the boundaries between the ordinary faithful and the gnostics on the other hand." (Deutsch, *Experientia*, I, 97).

[40.] The catechumens, from κατηχουμενος, *the one being instructed*. Smith noted "that catechumens may be left without full information—not to say misinformed—in order to protect their faith..." (*Clement*, 26). Flint: "The rite of baptism was full of echoes of an older world. Catechumens were exorcized several times as they approached the sacrament at which, finally, the Devil, father of the demons, was renounced." (*Witchcraft and Magic in Europe: Ancient Greece and Rome*, 335).

those *of Peter* (τα του Πετρου υπομνηματα),⁴¹ from which *he carried over into his first book* (μεταφερων εις το πρωτον αυτου βιβλιον)⁴² what was suitable for those progressing *step by step* (καταλληλα)⁴³ toward knowledge.

He composed *a more spiritual gospel* (πνευματικωτερον ευαγγελιον)⁴⁴ *for the use of those having attained perfection* (εις την των τελειουμενων χρησιν).⁴⁵ Nevertheless, he never *betrayed the ineffable* [mysteries] (αυτα τα απορρητα εξωρχησατο),⁴⁶ nor did he write down *the*

---

41. "The claim to have apostolic traditions was common in the ancient church…new apostolic traditions were discovered to settle new disputes as they arose, it must have been believed that the traditions had been secret before the time of their fortunate discovery." (*Clement*, 29). The υπομνηματα "refer to 'rough notes' or personal 'aides-memoire'" which would have remained in an unpolished state and circulated, if at all, among a closed circle of confidants. See Jay, *Journal of Early Christian Studies* 16 (2008): 578.

42. This would obviously make no sense unless there was at least one other edition of Mark.

43. *Step by step, one after another,* (LSJ, *A Greek-English Lexicon*, 899), a reference to the progression of the μυστης, *initiate*, into more advanced stages of the mysteries.

44. "…it contained or indicated more of the hidden sense of Jesus' teachings and actions." (*Clement*, 33).

45. From τελειος, *perfected* or *fully initiated,* whom Clement contrasts with the catechumens, those still in the process of having the secrets revealed.

46. The term εξορχεομαι, derived from ορχεομαι, *to dance* or *pantomime,* "was a common word for revealing the rites of the

hierophantic teaching (την ιεροφαντικην διδασκαλιαν)⁴⁷ of the Lord, but to those things already written, he added yet other deeds and still other sayings, the interpretation with which he was familiar, to initiate the hearers into the forbidden sanctuary⁴⁸ of the truth seven⁴⁹ times veiled. In this manner, in my opinion, he prepared them *neither grudgingly nor carelessly* (ου φθονερως ουδ' απροφυλακτως), and dying, he bequeathed his writing to the church in Alexandria, where even now *it is most carefully guarded* (ασφαλως ευ μαλα τηρειται),⁵⁰ being read *only before those who have*

---

mystery cults…and Clement uses it of them as well as of Christian mysteries." (*Clement*, 36).

47. From ιεροφαντης, *hierophant*, the expounder of sacred mysteries. "…Clement's polemic against pagan religion is most violent when he impugns the mystery religions. It is obvious that they were to him the only serious competition for Christianity, since they were still living religion, involving a personal relation of the individual believer to God…the competition of Christianity with the mysteries has influenced the form of the Christian religion itself most strongly…" (*Clement*, 38).

48. Magical tradition held that sacred books—ιερα βιβλος, "sacred book,"—were kept "in the innermost recess of the temple." (Daniel & Maltomini, *Supplementum Magicum*, II, 113).

49. Seven is a well-known magical number; scores of examples could be cited from the magical texts. Smith drew attention to similar imagery—the book with the seven seals—in Revelation 5:1 to which I would point out very similar imagery in Revelation 10:4.

50. The Alexandrian gnostics possessed "certain books which they were supposed to keep secret from the unworthy" but those books were sometimes "leaked." (*Clement*, 43). *Longer Mark* was

been initiated into the great mysteries (προς αυτους μονους τους μυουμενους τα μεγαλα μυστηρια).

Since the unclean demons are always scheming the destruction of the race of men, Carpocrates, having been taught by them and by employing *deceptive arts* (απατηλοις τεχναις), enslaved by those means a certain presbyter of the church in Alexandria and obtained from him *a copy of the mystical gospel* (απογραφον του μυστικου ευαγγελιου)[51] and interpreted it according to his blasphemous and carnal opinion. Moreover, he defiled the spotless and holy words, mixing them with shameless lies. The teachings of the Carpocratians are drawn out of this mixture.

Just as I have previously said, one must never yield to them as they expound their lies, nor concede that *the mystical gospel* (το μυστικον ευαγγελιον) was written by Mark, but rather deny it even under oath. For everything that is true is not spoken to all men. The

---

restricted to initiates; Theodore and members of his church, the Carpocratians—who may also have been members of Theodore's congregation, a church within a church—and Clement knew of the existence of the longer gospel. It was obviously known to the Alexandrian elect since it was read "before those who have been initiated into the greater mysteries." *Longer Mark* was an advanced ("mystical") edition, not a "secret" edition.

[51.] The term μυστικος (mustikos) means *having to do with the mysteries, secret*. In this case, however, μυστικος is defined in the context of the letter as "more spiritual," not "secret" (compare footnote 28 above).

wisdom of God declares through Solomon, "Answer the fool according to his foolishness," teaching that the light of truth is to be hidden from those who are mentally blind, and it also says, "from he who has not, it shall be taken away," and "let the fool walk in darkness." But we are sons of light, having been illuminated by the sunrise of the spirit of the Lord, for it says, "where the spirit of the Lord is, there is freedom."

To the clean, everything is clean. Therefore I will not hesitate to answer what you have asked, exposing their lies *from the very words of the Gospel* (δι' αυτων του ευαγγελιου λεξεων).[52] For instance, after "And they were in the road going up to Jerusalem," and what follows until "after three days he shall rise," it next says, *word for word* (κατα λεξιν), *"And they came to Bethany, and a certain woman whose brother had died came out and* **threw herself before Jesus** *(προσεκυνησε τον Ιησουν) and said to him, 'Son of David, have mercy on me.' But the disciples rebuked her. Becoming angry, Jesus went off after her into the garden where the tomb[53] was and suddenly there was*

[52.] The implication is that Clement regarded the "Secret" gospel as simply "the gospel" of Mark.

[53.] "Interpretation of the Lazarus story as foreshadowing Jesus' resurrection may have led to the location of Lazarus' tomb, too, in a κηπος [*garden*, my note]…The only reference to Jesus having raised a dead man from a tomb is in the Lazarus story, where μνημειον [tomb] occurs 3 times (Jn. 11.17, 31, 38) and is subsequently mentioned in the popular report of the miracle (12.17)." (*Clement*, 105).

heard coming from the tomb a loud voice.[54] *Approaching, Jesus rolled away the stone from the door of the tomb and immediately going into where the young man was, he stretched out his hand and raised him, holding his hand. And **gazing at him, the young man loved him** (ο δε νεανισκος εμβλεψας αυτω ηγαπησεν αυτον) and began to plead with him that he might be with him. And going from the tomb, they went into the young man's house, for he was rich. After six days,*[55] *Jesus summoned him and when evening came, the young man went to him **wearing a linen cloth** (περιβεβλημενος σινδονα) over his naked body and he stayed with him that night, for Jesus taught him the mystery of the kingdom*[56] *of God. And then, arising, he went to the far side of the Jordan.*

After this, it adds, "James and John went to him," and all that section, but "*naked man with naked man*" (γυμνος γυμνω) and the other things about which you wrote are not found. After "he goes into Jericho," it adds

---

[54]. Smith noted several parallels between the *Longer Mark* quotations and the Lazarus story: "φωνη μεγαλη [*loud voice*, my note]...the phrase is used in Jn. only once, in 11.43...Since the phrase was not a common element in John's vocabulary but was in Mark's, John is more likely to have derived it from a Markan story of the raising of Lazarus...the λιθος [stone] closing the entrance of the μνηνμειον [tomb] appears also in Jn.'s raising of Lazarus (11.38ff)..." (*Clement*, 107).

[55]. "After six days," or in other words, on the seventh day?

[56]. The gospel of Mark **refers** to a singular mystery of the kingdom (Mark 4:11) where the other synoptics read "mysteries." Koester argues that "mysteries" was the original reading.

only, "*and the sister of the young man who Jesus loved*[57] *and his mother and Salome were there, but Jesus did not agree to see them.*"[58] But the many other things about which you wrote[59] appear not to be, and are not, true. According to the true philosophical explanation..."

At this point the text breaks off.

[57.] "It has often been argued from Johannine evidence that the unnamed "beloved disciple" was Lazarus...The longer text strengthens the argument by first telling a version of the Lazarus story in which the dead youth's sister plays an important role and the youth is said to have loved Jesus, and then locating shortly after this a reference to the disciple whom Jesus loved and his sister." (*Clement*, 119).

[58.] According to the canonical gospel, Jesus refused to see his family when they attempted to take him under their control (Mark 3:31-35). As Brown notes, "a reader might infer that the sister and mother want to take the young man [νεανισκος, *neaniskos*, my note] back home..." (Brown, *Mark's Longer Gospel*, 155). Bauckham, assuming the Marcan fragments to be genuine, concluded "that the redactor [of *Longer Mark*, my note] has in mind Mark 3:31-35, where Jesus' mother (unnamed) and his brothers come to see Jesus and he (implicitly) refuses to receive them. A repetition of this incident must have seemed to the redactor the simplest way of introducing a reference to Jesus' mother accompanied by two other women into the narrative of Mark." (Bauckham, *Novum Testamentum* 33 (1991): 274-275.

[59.] The two passages quoted by Clement were apparently not the only subjects of Theodore's inquiry. "...we should no longer view the editing of Secret Mark to produce Canonical Mark as the mere excision of one or two offending passages." (Sellew,

Some who argue that Clement's letter is a forgery have claimed that the letter stops in a very convenient way since the forger does not have to invent a "true philosophical explanation." Obviously other possibilities exist: the person who copied the letter was more interested in the gospel quotations it preserved and the circumstances which led Clement to quote them, but was less interested in his disquisition on their meaning. Or the manuscript from which the copy was made was old and damaged and the relevant text missing, a situation common in ancient exemplars. Or, as suggested to me by Roger Viklund,[60] the "true philosophical explanation" was censored lest the wrong people read it. There existed a powerful taboo against the revelation of mysteries as this excerpt from a slander spell shows: "For I come proclaiming the slander of the defiled and unholy woman [Name], for she slandered your holy mysteries by revealing them to men..."[61]

Clement describes *Longer Mark* as an advanced text, read only before initiates. The restricted nature of the text is completely in keeping with the attitudes of his era. Regarding sacred books kept in secret places, Daniel and Maltomini note, "such claims are a well-known topos" of magical texts and cite a number of examples from the papyri.[62]

Naturally it has been objected that no original manuscript of the Clement letter exists. This, of course, is true. It is also true

---
The Future of Early Christianity, 253).
[60.] Viklund, personal communication, April, 2009.
[61.] Preisendanz, *Papyri Graecae Magicae* IV, 2476-2478.
[62.] Daniel & Maltomini, *Supplementum Magicum* II, 72-73.

that *no original manuscript of any book of the New Testament exists* nor, for that matter, of any ancient author, but to the best of my knowledge no Christian scholars have rejected the text of the New Testament on those grounds.

The copy of the Clement letter was written by hand, i.e., *it is a manuscript*, inscribed in the back of a printed book, a book already over 300 years old when Smith examined it in 1958. That the text was copied into the end pages of a printed book likely reflects the scarcity of paper in an isolated monastery during the era in which it was copied—Smith noted "extensive handwritten passages" on "binders' pages at front and back, blank pages between chapters, even margins…"[63] in the books he examined. To date no evangelical distinguished professor from a backwoods Bible college has thought of accusing Smith of forging random marginalia in multiple books, but there is always hope that such an egregious oversight may still be addressed.

Could a portion of a letter written by Clement of Alexandria in the 3rd century have survived at Mar Saba until the 18th century? That is clearly possible. The Dead Sea Scrolls were nearly two thousand years old when found sealed in clay jars that had been hidden in caves around the time of the First Jewish War. The Nag Hammadi trove, discovered in the 20th century, was likely buried in the Egyptian desert sometime in the 4th century. Tens of thousands of papyrus fragments from

---

[63.] Smith, *The Secret Gospel*, 10. Smith catalogued 489 books in the library, of which 96 were manuscripts or contained "significant manuscript additions in a variety of languages." (Pantuck, *Ancient Gospel or Modern Forgery?*, 204).

Oxyrhynchus survived for well over a millennium buried in a garbage dump! Given favorable climatic conditions, documents can survive for extended periods of time.

Did any scholar besides Smith see the Clement letter *in situ* before it disappeared? After discussing the presence of witnesses to the physical existence of the pages Smith photographed, Charles Hedrick concluded,

> The letter of Clement does exist, and the consensus (with some dissenting opinions) is that it is genuine. Thus at the end of the second century multiple different versions of the Gospel of Mark were known to exist. Scholars have been reluctant to accept Clement's testimony and assign the fragments of the Secret Gospel to the hand of the author of original Mark. But in spite of their reluctance, clearly Clement's letter confirms that a second Gospel of Mark thought to be by the author of the original Gospel of Mark was used in the Alexandrine Church, and it is to be dated before the end of the second century.[64]

Several experts on the subject of early gospels believe that *Longer Mark* was the original gospel of Mark and that text was subtracted from it, arriving at the present form of the gospel, (basically the position of Helmut Koester). Which is chicken and egg need not detain us here.[65] Clement contrasted Mark's

---

[64.] Hedrick, *The Fourth* R 13/5 (2000): 3-11, 14.

[65.] On the *status quaestionis* see Brown (*Journal of Biblical Literature* 122 (2003): 89-110), Sellew (*The Future of Early Christianity*, 242-

"more spiritual gospel" with an initial composition, "his first book," which indicates that Mark produced more than one edition of his gospel.

The 4th century church historian Eusebius cites one of Clement's lost writings, the *Hypotyposeis*, on the composition of the gospels: "he said of the gospels that *those first published* (προγεγραφθαι) included the genealogies."[66] The verb in question, προγραφω, has generally been understood to mean *written before*, but can also mean *display publicly* and is used in that sense in Galatians[67] where Jesus' crucifixion is described as a *public display*. A case can be made that the genealogical gospels were not written first, but that they were published first, i.e., Matthew and Luke were the first official, public biographies.[68] This reading of the evidence is supported by the context of Eusebius' report that says of Mark's gospel, "the gospel was shared by those who requested it."[69] The implication is that Mark was not initially a public gospel, but circulated hand to hand within a constricted circle of readers. Brown concludes "that longer Mark never circulated outside Alexandria except in its Carpocratian form, which postdated Matthew…longer Mark was an Alexandrian expansion of the canonical gospel by an author who had independent access to oral traditions also used in the Gospel of John."[70]

---

257), Smith (*Clement of Alexandria*, 280).
[66] Eusebius, *Ecclesiastical History* VI, 14.5.
[67] Galatians 3:1.
[68] Carlson, *New Testament Studies* 47 (2001): 118-125.
[69] Eusebius, *Ecclesiastical History* VI, 14.6.
[70] Brown, *Mark's Other Gospel*, 99, 120.

Hugh Humphrey has proposed "that the Gospel we now have is the synthesis of several stages of composition and written, plausibly, in different locations…The consequence of joining the first account with the second account [a passion narrative, my note] does result in 'a more spiritual Gospel.' Indeed, that is the result of the analysis I pursue here, which suggests that two originally independent accounts, one of them being of Jesus' passion and death, were joined…"[71]

Mark's relatively scant attestation in the papyri may also reflect limited circulation of the canonical gospel. There are twenty-four papyri (by my count) that are witnesses to Matthew, of which no less than twelve are tentatively assigned to some part of the 3rd century, as opposed to three papyri from the same period that preserve samples of Mark, only one of which, 𝒫45, is dated from the 3rd century. Regarding the use of Mark by early Christians, Smith observed, "…although no special connection to the Carpocratians is reported, the Gospel according to Mark was the most popular of the canonical gospels with the Gnostics in general (which may account for its comparative neglect by the orthodox)."[72]

The pages on which the letter to Theodore was found were removed from the book and subsequently "misplaced." Piovanelli had this to say about the treatment of irreplaceable documents by the Middle Eastern monasteries and museums where it has been their fate to end up:

> Comme nous le verrons, l'édition de Voss fut déplacée

[71.] Humphrey, *From Q to "Secret" Mark*, 25, 34.
[72.] Smith, *Clement of Alexandria*, 16.

> et restaurée en 1977 et, depuis cette date, on a perdu toute trace des deux feuillets de garde contenant la *Lettre à Théodore*. Toutefois, en ce qui concerne le destin fort capricieux parfois reservé aux manuscrits anciens, même dans institutions apparemment audessus de tout soupçon, il ne faut pas oublier, par example, que le célèbre codex d'Akhmim contenant les fragments grecs du *Livre d'Hénoch*, de l'*Évangile de Pierre* et de l'*Apocalypse de Pierre* (P. Cair.10759) est lui aussi actuellement "impossible à localizer" au Musée copte du Caire!"[73]

As of this writing, the majority of Clement experts appear to have accepted the authenticity of the letter to Theodore and some experts on the history of the gospels, notably Helmut Koester—"The piece of Secret Mark fits the Markan trajectory so well that a forgery is inconceivable"[74]—and Ron Cameron have long accepted the authenticity of the gospel fragments. The narrative fit was also noted by Meyer: "the Markan account simply reads in an easier and more natural manner when the special materials of the Secret Gospel are allowed to function within the story line. Canonical Mark is more abrupt, more opaque at key points, as we should anticipate in a document from which important passages have been removed."[75] For Meyer, "the longer text of Mark now makes better sense."[76]

[73.] Piovanelli, *Revue Biblique* 114 (2007): 63-64.
[74.] Quoted by Smith (*Harvard Theological Review* 75 (1982): 459).
[75.] Meyer, *Secret Gospels*, 117.
[76.] Meyer, *Ancient Gospel or Modern Forgery?*, 148.

It is my guess that Matthew and Luke copied from the edition Brown calls *Longer Mark* from which material was excised to produce the present form of Mark. There is at least one ancient source that alludes to variant copies of Mark; Origen mentions an otherwise unknown Lebes, a tax farmer, "not numbered among the apostles *except according to certain copies of the gospel according to Mark* (ει μη κατα τινα αντιγραφων του κατα Μαρκον ευαγγελιον)."[77] The letter to Theodore is only part of the evidence for varying editions of the first gospel— as Smith noted, Matthew and Luke can also be considered expanded editions of Mark—but it appears impossible that a definitive history of the text can be reconstructed from the surviving evidence. (The debate over the ending of Mark, which is well known, implies that we cannot make a firm determination of authenticity even on the basis of manuscript evidence.) After a study of their writings, Mullins concluded "that both Papias and Clement thought that Mark wrote an early gospel account and then added to it later" and is of the opinion that the longer gospel was likely "Secret" Mark.[78]

Clement clearly accused the Carpocratians of magical practice —they inveigled an elder of the Alexandrine church to secure a copy of *Longer Mark* "by employing *deceptive arts (απατηλοις τεχναις)*." Given the context, Clement obviously had in mind magic using demonic *paredroi*, agreeing with Irenaeus on that point:

[77.] Origen, *Contra Celsum* I, 62. Compare Mark 2:14.
[78.] Mullins, *Vigiliae Christianae* 30 (1976): 192.

[The Carpocratians] also perform *magical arts* and *enchantments* (τεχνας...μαγικας...επαοιδας), *potions and erotic spells* (φιλτροι και χαριτησια), and use *magical assistants* and *messengers of dreams* (παραδρους και ονειροπομπους) and other such evil works, *alleging they* already *have authority* to be the masters *of the princes* [or archons] (φασκοντες εξουσιαν εχειν...των αρχωντων) and the creators of this world.[79]

Like the broader culture in which it arose, the early church pullulated exorcists and miracle workers, crawled with magicians and prophets, and spawned a race of congenital liars and grifters, phonies and frauds, that flourishes unabated to this day.

---

[79] Irenaeus, *Adversus Haereses* I, 25, 3.

SMITH'S INTERPRETATION

Two features of Smith's interpretation in particular have drawn the heaviest fire: his brief speculation that spiritual union with Jesus may have included physical union and that this union might have taken place during a nude baptismal ritual. Since Smith's detractors *always* (as far as I'm aware) *start from Smith's interpretation of the letter rather than the letter itself*, these two parts of his analysis are worth briefly examining.

"Gaying" Jesus?

The frame revealed by the restoration of the fragment from *Longer Mark* consists of looks of mutual love—the gaze as a *coup de foudre* lurks within the text, but is not essential to understanding it. However, the parallelism between the two passages is too obvious to miss:[80]

> ο δε Ιησους εμβλεψας αυτω ηγαπησεν αυτον (Mark 10:21)

> ο δε νεανισκος εμβλεψας αυτω ηγαπησεν αυτον (*Longer Mark*)

> Jesus looked at him [the young man] and loved him...

---

[80] Smith noted Mark's tendency to establish identity "by the use of identical phrases." (*The Secret Gospel*, 64).

the young man looked at him [Jesus] and loved him...

While it is true that the canonical gospel of Mark does not specify the age of the man who met Jesus on the road to Jerusalem, the parallel account in Matthew twice specifies that he was a young man—it is probable that both *Longer Mark* and Matthew preserve the earliest tradition in this case, namely that the man who met Jesus on the road was both *young*[81] and *rich*.[82]

The conclusion that most enraged the Jesus Studies establishment was that the initiation Jesus sponsored may have involved physical union between Jesus and select disciples following a nude baptismal ritual. The offending passage, taken from Smith's popular description of his find, reads:

> It was a water baptism administered by Jesus to chosen disciples, singly and by night. The costume, for the disciple, was a linen cloth worn over the naked body. This cloth was probably removed for the

---

[81]. "the *young man* (νεανισκος) said to him, 'I have observed all these things...'" (Matthew 19:20); "when the *young man* (νεανισκος) heard what [Jesus] said, he went away offended..." (Matthew 19:22).

[82]. The parallel account of the young man on the road in Luke 18:18 calls him an αρχων (archōn), *ruler*, possibly "a wealthy Judean aristocrat from a suburb of Jerusalem," (Fowler, "Identification of the Bethany Youth," *Journal of Higher Criticism* 5/1 (1998): 3-22), the "other disciple" who accompanied Peter and went with Jesus into the courtyard of the high priest while Peter waited outside the gate (John 18:15-16).

baptism proper, the immersion in water, which was now reduced to a preparatory purification. After that, by unknown ceremonies, the disciple was possessed by Jesus' spirit and so united with Jesus. One with him, he participated by hallucination in Jesus' ascent into the heavens, he entered the kingdom of God, and was thereby set free from the laws ordained for and in the lower world. Freedom from the law may have resulted in completion of the spiritual union by physical union. This certainly occurred in many forms of gnostic Christianity; how early it began there is no telling."[83]

As Dale Martin notes,

> Smith suggested the fragment [of *Longer Mark*, my note] constituted evidence of ancient accounts of naked initiatory rites performed by Jesus himself with select male disciples, and Smith did not demur from opining that some homosexual activity may have constituted part of those initiations. Whatever one may think of Smith's hypothesis, one must admit that it would solve some conundrums. The significance of the naked young man in the canonical Gospel of Mark is just one such problem. Perplexing parallels between the Gospels of Mark and John constitute another. And Jesus of Smith's reconstruction would go a long way toward explaining why Jesus may have never married.[84]

[83.] Smith, *The Secret Gospel*, 106-107.
[84.] Martin, *Sex and the Single Savior*, 96.

It would appear from the context of the letter to Theodore that the Carpocratians interpreted Jesus' love as sexual, otherwise there would have been no point to the question regarding "naked man with naked man, (γυμνος γυμνω)"[85] and the scandal implied. Surely those scholars who accused Smith of inventing a scurrilous and baseless interpretation of an early Christian rite are aware of Clement's quotations of the gnostic Theodotus: "The Savior taught the apostles, at first *figuratively* (τυπικως) and *mystically* (μυστικως), later by parables and riddles, and third, *clearly and nakedly* (σαφως και γυμνως) *when they were alone* (κατα μονας)."[86] Did Theodotus understand the nakedness to be literal or metaphorical? At this remove, no one knows.

Since the release of *Clement of Alexandria*, the publication of the *Gospel of Judas* has added a further accusation of same-sex ritual made by Christians against other Christians.[87] When first discovered in a tomb in the late 1970's the codex was likely in a nearly pristine state of preservation, but owing to the greed and incompetence of the antiquities looters into whose hands it fell, it was fragmentary and close to complete disintegration by the time a responsible party acquired it. In spite of painstaking efforts at restoration, approximately 15% of *Judas* is either missing or illegible, and the true reading of several key passages remains unsure.

The specialists who have commented at length on the discovery appear cautious to a fault about exploring the

---

[85]. Compare the text of the letter (page 22).
[86]. Clement, *Excerpta ex Theodoto* 4.66.1.
[87]. See Conner, *Magic in Christianity: From Jesus to the Gnostics*, 32-35.

implications of any literal reading of the portion of the text that mentions men who "sleep with men." Pagels and King, for instance, acknowledge that the author of *Judas* is charging other Christians with "same-sex relations" but conclude that the various charges are "so outrageous that they cannot be taken literally."[88] Nevertheless, they consider the charge that Christians were sacrificing their wives and children to reflect the proto-orthodox enthusiasm for martyrdom and cite passages from the letters of Ignatius to support their contention. According to this interpretation, the charges of sacrificing women and children are not simply empty rhetoric —those slain by the wicked priests represent the martyrs who are being actively encouraged to die for the faith.[89] But if the accusations of human sacrifice reflect real fatalities, might the accusations of same-sex behavior also reflect real sexual practices?

Ehrman, who does an admirable job of drawing attention to the ambiguity of early Christian texts in which theological considerations outweigh any pretense of historical reportage, basically collapses the charges of same-sex behavior in *Judas* into the category of "sexual immorality," while pointing out that the orthodox hierarchy is being accused of various atrocities.[90] The editors of *The Gospel of Judas* dismiss the accusation of same-sex relations as "a standard feature of polemical argumentation."[91] Jenott, who has written a

---

[88] Pagels & King, *Reading Judas*, xii, 64-65, 137..
[89] Ibid, 53-56, 67-68.
[90] Ehrman, *The Lost Gospel of Judas Iscariot*, 112, 137.
[91] Kasser, et al., *The Gospel of Judas*, 195, 199.

meticulous analysis of *Judas* and the opinions swirling around it, notes that *Judas* "demonizes the apostolic cult," and points out that the tract is a product of ecclesiastical politics that even in the 2nd century had reached an incandescent pitch. Jenott also dismisses the charge of same-sex behavior as part of a "traditional list of slanderous tropes."[92] Reading the spate of recent books on *Judas* might leave the reader with the impression that the charge of sacrificing people may reflect deaths due to martyrdom, but the charge of same-sex behavior is simply too *outré*, an empty piece of vilification that needs no further scrutiny, an example "of mudslinging in antiquity."[93]

The Coptic text in question reads ϨⲚⲔⲞⲞⲨⲈ ⲈⲨⲚⲔⲞⲦⲔⲈ ⲘⲚ Ⲛ̄ϨⲞⲞⲨⲦ in which the verb, ⲚⲔⲞⲦⲔ (*to sleep*) plus the preposition ⲘⲚ (*with*) is a euphemism for sexual intercourse.[94] It is the same expression used in the Coptic version of Genesis 39:10 and Leviticus 18:22 where the meaning is clearly "to sleep with" in order to engage in sexual relations. The text literally breaks down as follows: ϨⲚ̄ (some) ⲔⲞⲞⲨⲈ (others) ⲈⲨⲚ̄ⲔⲞⲦⲔⲈ (they sleep) ⲘⲚ̄ (with) Ⲛ̄ (the) ϨⲞⲞⲨⲦ (males). The text is a clear, if euphemistic, accusation of same-sex activity made by Christians against other Christians but does it reflect reality, and if so, how would we know?

Regarding the Carpocratians specifically, Epiphanius claimed,

---

[92.] Jenott, *The Gospel of Judas*, 25, 26, 40, 58.
[93.] Gathercole, *The Gospel of Judas*, 77.
[94.] Kasser, et al., *The Gospel of Judas*, 195.

"...these people perform every kind of pederasty[95] and the most salacious sexual intercourse with women in every part of the body, and carry out *magic* (μαγαιας) and *witchery* (φαρμακειας) and idolatry."[96] It is possible, as commonly assumed, that Epiphanius is engaging in defamation with scant basis in fact. However it is also possible that he is providing specifics that Irenaeus was too prudish to specify.

Describing those the gnostics called "Levites," Epiphanius bluntly states, "Those they call 'Levites' *do not have intercourse with women, but have intercourse with each other* (ου μισγονται γυναιξι αλλα αλληλοις μισγονται), and those are persons they regard as the elect, indeed, the exalted ones."[97]

Origen quotes the pagan Celsus as claiming that "other [Christians], *invented a guardian* (ευραντο προστατην) for themselves by wickedly conceiving of *a master and tutelary spirit* (διδασκαλον τε και δαιμονα), and wallow about in utter darkness more lawless and more depraved than [the rites] *of those devoted to the Egyptian Antinous...*"(των Αντινου του κατ' Αιγυπτον θιασωτων).[98] It seems clear that the rites of Antinous, the favorite of Hadrian, particularly his "sacred

---

[95.] Epiphanius employs a late and uncommon word, ανδροβασια, a synonym of παιδεραστια, *boy love* (See Sophocles, *Greek-English Lexicon of the Roman and Byzantine Periods*, 158). His choice of words may reflect the fact that the latter still carried positive connotations among pagans and that the sexual relations he describes were between adults of equal age and status.

[96.] Epiphanius, *Panarion*, Book I, XXVII, 3.1, 4.6-7.

[97.] Ibid, Book I, XXVI, 13.1.

[98.] Origen, *Contra Celsum* V, 63.

nights," scandalized Christians and were, by implication, "flagrant and uninhibited homosexual orgies."[99] However, no copy of Celsus' work is extant. "Not a single copy of Celsus's book survives, as every one was ordered destroyed by the Christian emperor Valentinian III and Archbishop Theodosius in 448. Early Christianity took great pleasure not just in the annihilation of anyone or anything deemed to be pagan, but in wiping out any trace of dissent from its own historical records…Under Christian rule [Celsus] believes, the lower classes would rise up, fired not by a new love or understanding of philosophy, but inspired by a blind and unquestioning faith that actually revels in the ignorance of its adherents."[100]

As Smith pointed out, antinomianism has long existed in Judeo-Christian ranks, particularly at those points where believers have found themselves *in media res* theologically. One might cite as examples the Shabbatean movement in Judaism, Clarkson's preaching in 17th century England, or Puritans in the American colonies who "insisted that good works were pointless and a good life useless."[101] That an antinomian faction thrived in gnostic circles is well established —"amoralism is the means by which freedom is to be attained."[102] The gnostic is "a new kind of man who is subjugated neither by the obligations nor the criteria of the

---

[99] Lambert, *Beloved and God: The Story of Hadrian and Antinous*, 186-187.

[100] Pollard & Reid, *The Rise and Fall of Alexandria*, 210-211, 214.

[101] Armstrong, *The Battle for God*, 76.

[102] Jonas, *The Gnostic Religion*, 273.

present world of creation."[103] For a more complete analysis of sexual metaphor as well as accusations of sexual ritual in primitive Christianity see *Magic in Christianity: From Jesus to the Gnostics*.[104]

It is possible that Carpocrates, not Morton Smith, first raised the vexed question of Jesus' sexuality, but in any case, that question can never be answered on the basis of surviving evidence and even if answered would ultimately be of no importance. What is clear is that early Christians—as well as one well-informed pagan—accused certain gnostic sects of same-sex activity as well as debauched coupling with women and there is no particular reason to think those allegations were all just empty rhetoric. That said, there is no reason to think that *Longer Mark* as quoted by Clement describes a sexual ritual, regardless of how the Carpocratians may have interpreted it or despite what they may have added to it by way of text or commentary to justify their ritual practice. It would appear that the mention of the Carpocratians and the nudity beneath the linen sheet suggested a baptismal ritual to Smith, since early Christians were baptized nude,[105] so we may ask ourselves what is the evidence for…

…a baptismal ritual of initiation?

It is well known that Smith interpreted "the greater mysteries" as a baptismal ritual, but it is on this point that his argument is

---

[103] Rudolf, *Gnosis*, 253.

[104] Conner, *Magic in Christianity: From Jesus to the Gnostics*, 25-40.

[105] Smith cites Hippolytus (*Apostolic Tradition* XXI, 5,11) in support of this conclusion (*Clement of Alexandria*, 65).

the weakest. Smith claimed that "to the ancients, baptism was an initiation—a τελετε, as Lucian said (*Peregrinus*, 11)."[106] However, Lucian merely says that Jesus was worshipped "because he introduced *this new cult* (καινην ταυτην τελετην) …"[107]—Lucian says nothing about baptism. Peter's admonition, "Repent and be baptized *every one of you*…" with the result that about 3000 people were converted[108] does not make a compelling case that baptism was a rite for an elite group of the gnostic elect. Indeed, it sounds like Christian missionaries were bagging their limit of converts *en masse* and moving on. No special rite of initiation is mentioned in the case of the eunuch baptized by Philip,[109] or Paul,[110] or the friends and family of Cornelius who begin speaking in tongues—*just as Peter begins to preach*—and are then promptly baptized.[111]

It is hard to believe that the disciples gathered around Jesus were the raw material out of which an elevated gnostic *élite* would be formed. It has been estimated that about 90% of the population in the 1st century was completely illiterate[112] and the New Testament specifically states of Peter and John that they were αγραμματος (agrammatos), "without letters," unable to read or write[113]—Peter betrays himself in the

---

[106.] Smith, *Clement of Alexandria*, 179.
[107.] Lucian, *Peregrinus*, 11.
[108.] Acts 2:38, 41.
[109.] Acts 8:36-38.
[110.] Acts 9:18.
[111.] Acts 10:24, 48, 11:15.
[112.] The position of William V. Harris, *Ancient Literacy*, 147-175.
[113.] Acts 4:13.

gospels by his rustic Galilean accent.¹¹⁴ Since Jesus' closest disciples were predominantly men who worked with their hands, an inability to read or write would have been completely in keeping with their time and station in life, a point conceded by Origen who says *"they had not received even the rudiments of learning (μηδε τα πρωτα γραμματα μεμαθηκοτας) even as the gospel records about them."*¹¹⁵ Origen reports the charge that Christians were known for their utter lack of education (απαιδευτοτατους) and ignorance (αμαθεστατους) and that they were "sorcerers" (γοητας) who gained converts by misdirection: "they set traps for complete yokels" (παλευομεν δε τους αγροικοτερους).¹¹⁶ Given the evidence of the gospels, the likelihood that an advanced gnostic ritual of mystical ascension traces back to Jesus might seem less probable.

Smith was not unaware that his evidence was thin. "Particularly surprising is the particular obscurity concerning Jesus' use of baptism. He himself was baptized; but the synoptics say nothing of his having baptized his followers, while the Fourth Gospel contradicts itself on this point…it says in 3:22 that he did baptize…but in 4:2 it adds καιτοι γε Ιησους αυτος ουκ εβαπτισεν αλλ' οι μαθηται αυτου…There is admittedly some doubt as to when Paul is talking about baptism…"¹¹⁷ The text Smith quotes in Greek specifies: *"Jesus himself did not baptize, but his disciples* [did]."

---

¹¹⁴· Matthew 27:73.
¹¹⁵· Origen, *Contra Celsum* I, 62.
¹¹⁶· Ibid, VI, 14.
¹¹⁷· Smith, *Clement of Alexandria*, 209, 213.

In any event, even the texts to which Smith appealed do not make his case: "Look, this man [Jesus] is baptizing and *everyone is going to him*."[118] What is being described is quite obviously *mass baptism*, open to *everyone*, not private nighttime initiation. Citing Acts 16:25-34 as an example of nocturnal baptism hardly helps Smith's case either.[119] The jailer, overwhelmed by Paul's magical delivery, is baptized on the spur of the moment, together with his "entire family" and "all in his house"[120] which almost certainly included children and may even have included slaves. There is no advanced gnostic initiation in sight here, regardless of the hour when the baptisms occurred. Similarly, the baptism of Lydia included "her household"[121]—"perhaps consisting of women engaged in business with her or her slaves and freed clientele…the presence of children is particularly problematic."[122]

At one point Smith speculated, "Clement's church may have practiced a second baptism by which the believer achieved true gnosis," but to his credit acknowledged that a consultant thought the second baptism hypothesis "unlikely."[123] Paul Achtemeier, in a review that was critical, but hardly unfair, said, "Characteristically, his arguments are awash in speculation. As an example, we may consider his account of

---

[118.] John 3:26.
[119.] Smith, *Clement of Alexandria*, 175.
[120.] Acts 16:31-33.
[121.] Acts 16:15.
[122.] Furguson, *Baptism in the Early Church*, 179.
[123.] Smith, *Clement*, 168.

Jesus' act of baptizing, itself nowhere mentioned in the Synoptics and denied in John (4:2)...[the conclusion that Jesus' administered a baptismal ritual] is reached despite the fact that the LT ["longer text," my note] does not mention any baptism, let alone any ritual connected with it, let alone any theological justification for such an imagined ritual."[124]

Scholars sympathetic to the authenticity of *Longer Mark* have made essentially the same observation: "Jesus, unlike John, was not a baptizer but a healer. The tradition, therefore, had no baptism-by-Jesus stories that could be used in their baptismal liturgies. But a story about a miraculous or physical raising from death could be used or created as a symbol for baptismal or spiritual raising from death."[125]

It is true that Mark 10:38-39 mentions baptism:

> Jesus said to them, "You do not know what you're asking! Can you drink the cup I drink, or be baptized with the baptism with which I am baptized?" They answered, "We can." Then Jesus said to them, "The cup that I drink, you will drink, and you will be baptized with the baptism with which I am baptized."

Given the context, which includes the third prediction of his death,[126] it is clear that a "baptism" into martyrdom is in sight; the baptism is no more a literal water immersion than the cup

---

[124.] Achtemeier, *Journal of Biblical Literature* 93 (1974): 627.
[125.] Crossan, *The Historical Jesus*, 330.
[126.] Mark 10:33-34.

is a literal cup. As noted by Edward Smith, *Longer Mark* and the parallel story in John concerns resurrection and teaching, not baptism. "Nothing in John's account gives any basis for thinking that a baptism was involved. This is important if John's version is the more reliable."[127]

Smith asked, "If this was not an initiation, what was the young man doing with Jesus at such an hour, in such a place, and in such a costume?"[128] I will argue, following the lead of others, that answers to those questions are present within the texts at hand, *answers that do not invoke either baptism or secret rites or sexual relations*. Be that as it may, it is essential to note that *Smith's opponents nearly always conflate his interpretation of the Clement letter with the question of authenticity*. It persistently escapes their notice that these are two separate, even unrelated, issues, and that even if one assumes Smith's interpretation was agenda-driven, that is still not sufficient to declare the letter to Theodore a forgery.

I regard the letter as authentic. It is my opinion that (1) the letter is not a forgery, (2) that the letter was written by Clement, and (3) that the fragments attributed to Mark were in fact written by the same hand that penned the gospel of Mark. Whether the canonical gospel of Mark resulted from the deletion of material from *Longer Mark* or whether the canonical gospel was the first edition to which material was added to create the mystical gospel is, in my opinion, moot. It

---

[127.] Smith, *The Temple Sleep of the Rich Young Ruler*, 211.
[128.] Smith, *Clement*, 237.

is my impression, however, that canonical Mark is probably an expurgated version of a longer original.

THE ACADEMY RESPONDS

Smith's analysis of his discovery and the conclusions he drew were very different from the preachments about Jesus in mainstream New Testament studies and they provoked a firestorm of invective and denial from Catholic and evangelical quarters, a reaction that has been masterfully summarized by Shawn Eyer.[129] Today, four decades after Smith published, opinion regarding the authenticity of his find is still divided along much the same lines; theological commitment, not textual or forensic evidence, is the best single predictor of which side of the "Secret" Mark debate any given individual will endorse—an agnostic following the details might well conclude that there is more evidence for the authenticity of *Longer Mark* than there is for the existence of God.

It should be pointed out to the reader who is incompletely familiar with the details of the "Secret" gospel saga that the arguments pro and con for authenticity have followed two basic tracks. Those who accept the Clement letter as genuine tend to support their position by concentrating on the text, fitting the Marcan fragments back into the canonical gospel to see (1) if the narrative arc makes better sense with the verses restored and (2) if any longstanding aporia in Mark are thereby resolved. Those who argue against authenticity tend to concentrate on Smith, claiming he forged the letter, and

---

[129.] Eyer, *Alexandria: The Journal for the Western Cosmological Tradition* 3 (1995):103-129.

seek to support their contention by (1) ascribing ulterior motives to Smith and (2) proving the letter is a forgery by using a series of forensic demonstrations centered on statistical analysis of the vocabulary and handwriting analysis. Based on my own study, I have long believed the Clement letter to be authentic—I'd put the probability of authenticity at 90%—and I will argue that having failed to discredit Smith's discovery on textual and linguistic grounds, the conservative camp has increasingly resorted to ad hominem attacks on Smith, focusing particularly on his alleged sexuality, and conspiracy theory. It is my opinion that the gospel fragments in the Clement letter were written by the same hand that composed the canonical gospel of Mark, that the Clement letter is genuine, and that arguments to the contrary have failed, in several cases having failed spectacularly.[130]

Very little of the response to Smith's interpretation was of any factual consequence. Most early reviewers, writing in sectarian publications, were intensely antagonistic to Smith's conclusions, his homoerotic reading of the evidence in particular, and were noisily venting their displeasure. Quentin Quesnell, one of the few writers who attempted a refutation on factual lines, strongly implied that the Clement letter and the lost gospel fragments it preserved were forgeries.[131] The

---

[130.] Roger Viklund has produced an accessible summary of the contours of the controversy (rogerviklund.wordpress.com/2011/01/30/refuting-the-gospel-hoax/).

[131.] Quesnell, *The Catholic Biblical Quarterly* 37 (1975), 48-67. Quentin Quesnell, a member of the Society of Jesus at the time of his rebuttal, left the order and, released from his vows, married. He died in 2012. In 2011, Timo Paananen published an

clear implication was that Smith had forged the letter to which Smith replied, "Quesnell...challenges the text solely because of its content. But other texts from the same library [a scholia of Sophocles, for example, my note] go unquestioned. But one should not suppose a text spurious simply because one dislikes what it says."[132] In time, several of Quesnell's talking points, particularly the claim that only Smith had seen the pages in question, were to prove baseless, and could, with very little imagination, be construed as deliberately deceptive. Seen in retrospect, Quesnell's article did little more than throw a dead cat in the well.

F. F. Bruce, a member of the conservative evangelical Plymouth Brethren, opined that the longer gospel fragment was "Marcan in diction, for the simple reason that it is largely a pastiche of phrases from Mark ('contaminated' by Matthean parallels), coupled with some Johannine material." Bruce also noted that the "raising of the young man of Bethany from the tomb at his sister's entreaty is superficially similar to the incident of the raising of Lazarus..."[133] As most beginning students of the New Testament are aware, each of the canonical gospels is itself a "pastiche" constructed from multiple sources. Luke, for example, is an appropriation of material from Mark, *Q*, and other, unknown, oral and written sources, clipped and pasted together to meet the author's objectives. Exactly how a pastiche per se might mark a gospel

---

exchange with Quesnell that was as brief as it was unrevealing (salainenevankelista. blogspot.com/2011/06/short-interview-with-quentin-quesnell.html).

[132.] Smith, *The Catholic Biblical Quarterly* 38 (1976): 196.

[133.] Bruce, *The 'Secret' Gospel of Mark*, 11.

or gospel fragment as inauthentic Professor Bruce did not venture to explain. Indeed, Dr. Bruce's response might be regarded by some as too clever by half since it inevitably opens the vexed question of how any pseudonymous document assembled from unknown sources a generation after the fact by a person who was not an eyewitness could possibly be regarded as telling the truth, the whole truth and nothing but the truth. However, none of these subtleties would have carried any weight for Bruce, who for his entire career remained committed to the historical reliability of the New Testament as a credendum.

Smith, whose analysis of the text of the Clement letter was fastidious, did not overlook the possibility that the Marcan fragments were a cento. Against the cento compositional theory Smith marshaled the following arguments that I will quote in severely abbreviated form: (1) "Some elements of the longer text are not paralleled from the canonical gospels…" (2) "…the parallels are brief formulas, most of them used many times in the canonical gospels…" (3) "to suppose it a cento, one must also suppose that the author derived his scraps from practically every chapter of Mk, to say nothing of the other gospels…" (4) "Many details of the text do not look as if they had been produced by the compiler of a cento [five examples are cited, my note]…" (5) "the text is too well constructed and economical to be a cento: there are no irrelevant details, every word comes naturally in its place, the narration moves without delays or jumps…" (6) "…the longer text is datable…and at this date Mk.'s prestige was not high enough to motivate this sort of imitation…" (7) "[in Dodd's examination of other fragmentary gospels such as P.

Egerton, my note] he found evidence that…the divergent forms of canonical stories…were probably also derived from non-canonical sources…Much of his reasoning therein is applicable, mutatis mutandis, to the present case…There is no passage of Clement's extant works from which [the letter] could have been derived by adaptation…it almost never uses Clement's exact words, though it constantly uses his vocabulary, his phraseology, and his metaphors."[134]

Occasional articles have appeared that reject the argument for authenticity on the grounds of statistical analysis of the vocabulary of the text.[135] The gist of the statistical argument appears to be that the letter contains too many words peculiar to Clement to have been written by Clement, a claim that effectively casts the analyst in the role of a clairvoyant who can perform a posthumous reading of Clement's mind. This tactic effectively sets an initial condition guaranteed to skew the results of the 'analysis' in a predetermined direction, its apparent purpose. Vocabulary analysis would seem particularly problematic in a writer like Clement who is well known for a style that freely mixes quotation, allusion and recall from memory with his 'own' words. Smith was completely aware of the intertextual tendency of Clement's prose—"multiple biblical allusion is typical of Clement"—and provides a number of examples of Clement's rampant borrowing in his analysis. Smith also noted that Clement tends to weave quotations and references to biblical texts into

---

[134] Smith, *Clement of Alexandria*, 143-144, 76.

[135] For example, Osborn in *The Second Century* 3.4 (1983): 219-244 and Criddle in *Journal of Early Christian Studies* 3 (1995): 215-220.

his writing so that "each line of thought is regularly associated with certain biblical passages."[136]

At this point another objection to the statistical analysis argument may be added: early witnesses to Clement are both sparse and defective. As observed by Cosaert, "only a handful of relatively late continuous text manuscripts exist today." The oldest known is the "badly mutilated" 10th century *Arethus Codex*, derived from "an exemplar full of textual corruptions, lacunae, interpolations, and dislocations." The *Codex Laurentianus*, the 11th century source for the text of the *Stromateis* and other works, "is full of textual corruptions, errors of names, numbers, omissions, misplaced sentences, as well as insertion of marginalia into the text…the manuscript evidence makes it impossible to rule completely out the possibility that Clement's citations were altered through the transmission process…"[137] It is upon these late, corrupted texts that the *soi disant* vocabulary analysis is ultimately based. Grafton has raised a further objection to the vocabulary analysis charade. Short of having all Clement's writings, one could never be sure what vocabulary Clement might have used. "In the absence of a complete corpus of his work—something we have for no ancient writer—how could we know, except by assuming what we want to prove?"[138]

Notwithstanding these fairly obvious hurdles, the purveyors of the statistical analysis hypothesis proceed as if the subject of their claim were a pristine text known with certainty to

---

[136.] Smith, *Clement of Alexandria*, 8, 18-19.
[137.] Cosaert, *The Text of the Gospels in Clement of Alexandria*, 13-14.
[138.] Grafton, *The Nation*, January 26, 2009, 26.

preserve the *ipsissima verba* of its author, one of several convenient assumptions designed to yield the desired answer to their inquiry. The defects of the sources aside, the shuttlecock of statistical methodology, debates about the finer points of analysis and meta-analysis, continues to be batted back and forth in their circle while the reliability of the text under examination is taken as given. Drawing dogmatic conclusions from a text with interpolations, errors, invasive marginalia and corruptions is in the very best case shoddy procedure, in a slightly worse case mere incompetence, and in the worst case, academic fraud pure and simple.

Aside from pointing out problems with the sources, I disclaim any competence when it comes to statistical analysis per se. I would, however, point to an article that has been completely ignored as far as I can tell among Smith's detractors. The piece, published in *The American Statistician* by Andrew Solow and Wollcott Smith,[139] is beyond my ability to clearly understand, much less critique. However, with the permission of Dr. Solow, I offer our email exchange regarding his impressions:

> Dear Dr. Solow,
>
> I am currently writing a book on "Secret" Mark for a publisher in the UK and ran across your article in *American Statistician*. I am certainly not a mathematician, unless by "mathematician" one means to say "innumerate." Naturally I had to take statistics

---

[139] Solow & Smith, "A Statistical Problem Concerning the Mar Saba Letter," *The American Statistician* 63.3 (2009): 254-257.

in college and passed with flying colors, which is sobering to contemplate seeing that I emerged looking pretty good and actually knowing bupkes, so I will not venture any questions about your meta-analysis of Criddle's work given that I would not understand your answer in any case.

However, two (or three) questions, if I may impose. First (the most interesting), what on Earth got a researcher in oceanography interested in the Mar Saba letter? Do you tend to accept or doubt the authenticity of the find overall based on your study, and in either case, how would such a statistical study of a text still apply unless the complete corpus of the writer in question were available for analysis?

Thank you for your time and attention. If I may, I'd like permission to share your observations with Roger Viklund who has a great interest in the Clement letter controversy and has blogged specifically (and way more intelligently than I could) about your article.

Best wishes,

Robert Conner

[Reply from Andrew Solow]:

Thanks for your message. In answer to your first question, I have an amateur (and non-religious) interest in New Testament history. I read about Criddle's paper in one of Bart Ehrman's book, looked it up, and just started fooling around with the technical aspects of the problem. My paper is only about these technical aspects with an interesting and unusual application. I am not in a position to have a strong opinion about authenticity. Although others have used word frequencies to address this general issue, I have an amateur's skepticism: writers are not word-generators who unwittingly follow simple rules of word choice. Birds and dolphins, maybe, but not humans.[140]

I suspect that the majority of New Testament scholars who have cited Criddle's article over the years know less about applications of statistics than they do about the anatomy of the spinal cord, but they found an opinion that supported what they believed, and although unable to evaluate the validity of the argument themselves, cited it without knowing whether it might be flawed or reductionist. People trained in the humanities, only too happy to refer to what statistics had "proven," were basically telling those on the opposite side of the issue, "Do the math!" Whether they themselves could do the math was irrelevant.

Whatever one may think about 'lies, damn lies, and statistics,' it seems clear that the authenticity of a short text like the letter to Theodore, widely conceded to be very similar in style and vocabulary to Clement's confirmed writings, simply

---

[140.] Exchange of emails, May 26, 2014.

cannot be excluded on the basis of statistical analysis no matter how sophisticated the method. Based on textual criticism of the gospels, for which there are thousands of samples, significant alteration during the transmission process is the only thing that can be confidently assumed *a priori* of any ancient document. It is past time that the statistical argument against authenticity be put permanently to bed.

Confronted with the hurdles of producing a spurious letter of Clement that duplicates the style of Clement, inserting into the letter fake fragments of Mark that closely copy the style of authentic Mark, and then reproducing the letter by hand in an 18th century Greek cursive in the back of a rare book, champions of the forgery hypothesis were forced to accuse Smith of being *fiendishly* clever, a backhanded compliment of which Smith made light. Impressive though his erudition was, I fail to find in Morton Smith a latterday reincarnation of Professor Moriarty. In fact, Smith's facility in Greek has now been examined by referencing both his surviving correspondence and the eyewitness testimony of scholars such as Roy Kotansky who was in a position to assess Smith's facility in Greek. Based on this new evidence it appears unlikely that Smith was capable of composing the Clement letter.[141]

The daunting technical and scholarly difficulties involved in forging such an ancient letter containing two very distinctive styles have led Bart Ehrman, who believes Smith possessed the skills necessary to commit such a forgery, but has never claimed he did so, to note:

[141.] Pantuck, *Ancient Gospel or Modern Forgery?*, 184-211.

It is true that a modern forgery would be an amazing feat. For this to be forged, someone would have to imitate an eighteenth-century Greek style of handwriting and to produce a document that is so much like Clement that it fools experts who spend their lives analyzing Clement, which quotes a previously lost passage from Mark that is so much like Mark that it fools experts who spend their lives analyzing Mark. If this is forged, it is one of the greatest works of scholarship of the twentieth century, by someone who put an uncanny amount of work into it.[142]

Elsewhere Ehrman has stated, "I don't think we can say whether or not Smith forged the letter. We won't know until, if ever, the manuscript is found and subjected to a rigorous investigation, including testing of the ink."[143] Smith himself said of the "imaginary genius" proposed by advocates of the forgery hypothesis, "The faith that could believe in such a man could move mountains. It would have mountains to move."[144] Another scholar closely connected to the controversy has unequivocally denied the possibility that the Clement letter was faked. "Morton Smith did not forge the manuscript…Smith simply could not have pulled off a forgery under the conditions at the monastery in 1958."[145]

However, in what seems to me a rather bizarre twist of

---

[142] Ehrman, *Lost Christianities*, 82.
[143] Ehrman, *Journal of Early Christian Studies* 11.2 (2003): 162.
[144] Smith, *Catholic Biblical Quarterly* 38 (1976): 197.
[145] Hedrick, *Journal of Early Christian Studies* 11.2 (2003): 140.

reasoning, Ehrman concluded that Smith might have spent a decade of work perpetuating an elaborate fraud that included writing two books for "the fun of it."[146] In the process of writing this book, I communicated with Professor Ehrman, briefly outlining my position on the attacks against Smith and received a terse reply: "It sounds like you are hostile to the idea that Smith may have forged it. I'm not."[147] I regard Ehrman as easily one of the leading New Testament scholars of his generation, and that said, I think his opinion on letter writing should count for something.

> There is nothing inherent in learning to read that can necessarily teach you how to write. I know this full well. I can read Greek, Hebrew, French, German, and a range of other languages, but I cannot compose a letter in any of these languages.[148]

Having read a number of Ehrman's books and several of Smith's, I can see no reason to think that Morton Smith was substantially smarter or better trained than Bart Ehrman, much less that Smith was able to compose a letter in Greek that imitated not one, but two distinct styles reflecting two markedly different linguistic registers.

Two important articles on the epistolary form as it applies to the letter to Theodore have appeared in the *Journal of Early Christian Studies*. In his *Gospel Hoax*, discussed in the next

---

[146.] Ehrman, *Lost Christianities*, 88.

[147.] Personal communication, May 22, 2014.

[148.] Ehrman, *Forged*, 72.

chapter, Stephen Carlson based some of his criticisms on supposed logical incongruities that he alleges betray the hand of a modern forger.[149] Those criticisms have now been rebutted, point-by-point, but two must be singled out for further mention.

The first, that the letter is addressed to a private individual but needlessly reiterates facts that person would already know, is invalidated if Theodore was a church official combating the Carpocratians, possibly within his own congregation(s). The Carpocratians supported their claims with the text of a corrupted gospel. The letter, although addressed to Theodore, would become an official document shared with a wider audience, "any academic interested in the topic,"[150] and would function as an internal church record that could be referenced even after Theodore's death. The letter's broader audience could not be presumed to have the same familiarity with Carpocratian claims as Theodore, the immediate recipient, hence the inclusion of background information already known to Theodore.

Brown also addresses the question of why Clement would quote *Longer Mark* "word for word" (κατα λεξιν) if Theodore already knew its contents. In fact, Clement uses κατα λεξιν twenty-four times in his confirmed writings, half of them "in connection with Christian writers whom Clement deemed heretical."[151] Clement's quotation thereby draws a careful

---

[149.] Carlson, *The Gospel Hoax*, 54-58.
[150.] Brown, *Journal of Early Christian Studies* 16 (2008): 540.
[151.] Ibid, 553.

distinction between the heretical Carpocration gospel and the authentic gospel held by the church in Alexandria to which it was bequeathed. In point of fact, Smith made the identical observation: "The κατα λεξιν formula or an equivalent was used by Clement particularly when quoting heretics…"[152] Smith then cites seven examples, a point overlooked by Carlson in his stampede to discredit Smith. Although I have not surveyed the early apologetic writings and admit to working from memory, I would point out that Eusebius also uses κατα λεξιν in his treatise against Apollonius of Tyana. Referring to Philostratus' biography, Eusebius says, "he asserts [the following], which I cite *verbatim* (κατα λεξιν)"[153]— it would appear that quoting *textually* from opponents was an early Christian polemical tactic.

In the second article, Jeff Jay compares the Clement letter with ancient correspondence written with similar intentions and concludes, "The letter to Theodore is plausible in light of letter writing in the late second or early third century and has tight generic coherence in form, content, and function."[154] In short, both studies confirm that the letter to Theodore fits the *Sitz Im Leben* originally identified by Smith.

By 1977 the Voss book had been removed from the monastery at Mar Saba and the handwritten pages separated from it. Both book and pages then disappeared, presumably due to carelessness on the part of the Greek Orthodox library

---

[152] Smith, *Clement of Alexandria*, 63.

[153] See Conybeare, *Philostratus: The Life of Apollonius of Tyana*, II, 538.

[154] Jay, *Journal of Early Christian Studies* 16 (2008), 573-597.

staff. Although the book turned up again in 2000, the handwritten pages are still conveniently missing. In 1980, Thomas Talley visited the Patriarchate library in Jerusalem, where the missing pages had been taken, but was told about the missing document, "qu'il était en cours de réparation," although why the pages would need "repair" was not stated. Eventually Charles Hedrick managed to secure color photos of the pages through the good offices of Nikolaos Olympiou who has suggested that the missing pages "were likely concealed by certain well-meaning persons at the Patriarchate library for reasons of piety."[155] In 2003, Guy Stroumsa belatedly added his testimony to the existence of the missing pages.[156]

In short, the end pages containing the letter have been removed, effectively preventing any further examination of the text or ink. The loss of the original has been rather graciously attributed to mere carelessness, or even to concerns over "piety," not surprising given the pseudo-scholarly hysterics Smith's interpretation continue to evoke. Lately we are assured that "The Patriarchate has no interest in [the "Secret" Mark] issue…"[157]

The visits of American scholars requesting to see the pages containing the *Longer Mark* text alerted the leadership of the Greek Orthodox Church that some within the academic community took the find seriously. Someone obviously

---

[155.] Hedrick & Olympiou, *The Fourth R* 13.5 (2000), 3-16.
[156.] Stroumsa, *Journal of Early Christian Studies* 11 (2003): 147-153.
[157.] Hedrick, *Ancient Gospel or Modern Forgery?*, 60.

ordered the book to be transferred from the library at Mar Saba to the Patriarchal library in Jerusalem where the offending pages were removed—it bears repeating that Morton Smith never had anything to do with restricting access to the Voss book. At this juncture several scenarios suggest themselves: the pages were stolen by someone who realized their potential value on the antiquities market, or church officials removed a sample of ink, had it tested by a forensic lab, and discovered to their dismay that the ink was not modern. If the latter, the finding would bolster the case for authenticity, so in the interest of avoiding further scrutiny, the hierarchy did what any competent heresy hunter would do: they destroyed the pages.[158] Or it is possible, given the demonstrated indifference of Middle Eastern religious libraries to the material in their possession,[159] that some sexually anxious monk destroyed the pages on his own. In any case, the Orthodox library could quickly clear itself of any suspicion of theft, negligence or vandalism by producing the pages.

The charge that the Greek Orthodox clergy may have

[158.] My suspicion that the pages have been destroyed is heightened by the fact that Agamemnon Tselikas, who knows the library and its personnel, "made every effort to find the pages, but he was unsuccessful." (Shanks, *Ancient Gospel or Modern Forgery?*, 138). The clear implication is that the pages simply no longer exist.

[159.] As many readers are likely aware, in 1844 Tischendorf discovered the monks of St. Catherine's using pages from the Codex Sinaiticus for kindling. It appears debatable how much monkish attitudes toward texts have improved in the interim.

permitted the destruction of a potentially invaluable witness to an early gospel edition might further darken the reputation of clerics already known to require the intervention of non-Christians to keep them from fighting with one another like junkyard dogs.[160] That said, it is possible that the Greek Orthodox eminences concocted a narrative claiming the pages were simply misplaced, a tale that unfortunately can only be confirmed by finding them. This story, however thin, casts the clergy in a somewhat less ominous light than a sullen refusal to allow scholars to see the contents of a library. As matters currently stand, those involved may be provisionally regarded as merely incompetent rather than criminally obstructive, but I tend to regard the latter conclusion as more likely. In a recently published collection of essays, Hedrick said, "I must confess that I do not understand the silence of the Greek Orthodox Patriarchate in this matter. Had a priceless antique manuscript in any other major library of the world gone missing and the ancient volume in which it was written damaged, at the very least there would have been a subsequent investigation and an official report made that could be released to interested members of the public."[161] As of this writing the pages that contain the text of the letter to Theodore have been missing for 37 years—since 1977—so it is probably not premature to declare them missing and presumed dead.

It is not my purpose to rehearse every argument for or against the authenticity of the Clement letter. Ehrman wrote a

---

[160.] http://videosift.com/video/Priests-fighting-in-the-Church-of-the-Holy-Sepulchre.

[161.] Hedrick, *Ancient Gospel or Modern Forgery?*, 43.

skeptical summation of the evidence for and against in 2003, but conceded, "At the outset, however, I should emphasize that the majority of scholars Smith consulted while doing his research were convinced that the letter was authentic, and probably a somewhat smaller majority agreed that the quotations of Secret Mark actually derived from a version of Mark. Even today, these are the majority opinions."[162] Ten years after the publication of the Mar Saba letter, Smith revealed that twenty-five experts attributed it to Clement, four did not, and six had no opinion.[163] Meyer wrote a collection of essays that represent another source of analysis of the controversies surrounding the "Secret" Gospel,[164] and Crossan's *Four Other Gospels* contains additional valuable commentary.[165]

However, the standard by which all future work on *Longer Mark* will measured in Scott Brown's *Mark's Other Gospel*,[166] published in 2003, a redaction and expansion of his doctoral dissertation,[167] the first ever written on the subject of Smith's discovery. Brown's book and subsequent defense of his work has moved the debate to considerably higher ground, cutting through forty years of scholarly "folklore," removing "the

---

[162.] Ehrman, *Lost Christianities*, 67-89.
[163.] Smith, *Harvard Theological Review* 75 (1982): 449-461.
[164.] Meyer, *Secret Gospels: Essays on Thomas and the Secret Gospel of Mark*.
[165.] Crossan, *Four Other Gospels: Shadows on the Contours of Canon*.
[166.] Brown, *Mark's Other Gospel: Rethinking Morton Smith's Controversial Discovery*.
[167.] Brown, *The More Spiritual Gospel: Markan Literary Techniques in the Longer Gospel of Mark*.

weak, the misinformed, the fanciful, and the intellectually dishonest arguments,"[168] of which there have been many. In a summary of the arguments to that point, Piovanelli wrote regarding Brown's work, "Cet ouvrage retrace d'une façon tellement exhaustive, scrupuleuse, exacte et, dans la mesure du possible, impartiale l'histoire des études consacrées à la *Lettre à Theodore* et à l'*Èvangile secret de Marc*, qu'il force l'admiration de tous ses lectures et ses lectrices."[169]

Since his apparent endorsement, Piovanelli has changed sides. He now advances the argument that Smith's interpretation of *Longer Mark* functioned "to reduce the historical Jesus to the status of a libertine miracle-worker…to make a stronger proposal about the historical Jesus as a miracle-worker/magician, [Smith] was in need of more consistent proof."[170] This seems to me an extraordinarily disingenuous line of attack. No doubt Dr. Piovanelli is aware that Jesus' Jewish contemporaries and pagans of the era accused both him and his followers of practicing magic—"common Jewish people considered Jesus a μαγος."[171] Origen's *Contra Celsum* is an extended defense against the charge that Jesus learned magic in Egypt[172] and that he was an evil sorcerer, hated by God.[173] Modern claims for magical praxis in the career of

---

[168] Brown, *Mark's Other Gospel*, 71.

[169] Piovanelli, *Revue Biblique* 114 (2007): 240.

[170] Piovanelli, *Ancient Gospel or Modern Forgery?*, 160.

[171] Eitrem, *Some Notes on the Demonology in the New Testament*, 41.

[172] Origen, *Contra Celsum*, I, 28.

[173] Ibid, I, 71.

Jesus date back at least to Bonner's article in 1927,[174] followed by Samain's in 1932,[175] Kraeling's in 1940,[176] and Eitrem's essay in 1966,[177] long before Smith wrote *Jesus the Magician*.[178] Hull's classic, *Hellenistic Magic and the Synoptic Tradition*, released in 1974, predated Smith's book by four years. Magical practice in Judaism had been acknowledged at least as far back as Trachtenberg in 1939.[179]

By the time Smith published his "Secret" Mark material, historians of the era had acknowledged that Jesus employed magical techniques in his exorcisms and healings, at least those scholars not sniffing the glue of theology. Smith hardly needed to produce an elaborate forgery to support his contention that the "historical Jesus"—whatever that means —and his followers were widely, if not universally, perceived by their contemporaries as magicians. Nor do I regard it as very likely that a man who labored over two Ph.D.'s would risk being drummed out of the academy, losing both his livelihood and reputation while simultaneously betraying his colleagues, simply to make a point. Although Smith references *Clement of Alexandria* in *Jesus the Magician*, the references are

---

[174.] Bonner, "Traces of Thaumaturgic Technique in the Miracles," *Harvard Theological Review* 20 (1927): 171-181.

[175.] Samain, "L'accusation de magie contre le Christ dans les évangiles," *Ephemerides Theologicae Lovanienses* 15 (1932): 449-490.

[176.] Kraeling, "Was Jesus Accused of Necromancy?" *Journal of Biblical Literature* 59 (1940): 147-157.

[177.] Eitrem, *Some Notes on the Demonology in the New Testament*.

[178.] *Jesus the Magician* was released in 1978.

[179.] Trachtenberg, *Jewish Magic and Superstition*.

largely confined to his endnotes along with scores of other sources.

In any event, the several lines of evidence Brown cites in support of authenticity and his subsequent defense of his conclusions against challengers are too extensive to be rehashed here. It must suffice to say that I found the evidence for authenticity compeling, even while disagreeing with Smith's baptismal interpretation, well before the publication of Dr. Brown's analysis. I find myself in agreement with Brown on several key points, particularly his evaluation of Smith: "[Smith] was a brilliant and erudite scholar, but he did not comprehend the Letter to Theodore well enough to have composed it."[180] I agree that Smith did not completely appreciate how the restored verses change the narrative trajectory of canonical Mark.

In a recent assessment of Smith's work, Amanda Porterfield says, "Smith made an important contribution to the historical study of Jesus by drawing attention to Jesus' work as a charismatic performer. But his impatience with the theological influences shaping historical studies of Jesus resulted in a draconian agenda to debunk theological claims and cut Jesus down to size." Smith wrote as a historian whose work, as Porterfield correctly notes, placed Jesus "in the context of comparative religion."[181] It is a constant item on the whine list of believers that *Morton Smith was insufficiently deferential both to the Lord Jesus and to other scholars.* That Smith was not credulous, an apologist for Christianity, did not gladly suffer those he

---

[180.] Brown, *Mark's Other Gospel*, 74.
[181.] Porterfield, *Healing in the History of Christianity*, 28.

considered fools, and pointed out that Jesus' "charismatic" performances were understood by his Jewish contemporaries and pagans alike as the work of a magician and a fraud, at best convicts him of *religionsgeschichliche*.

In some quarters impatience with theological claims masquerading as history is seen as basic to the historical method only so long as the rejection of such claims does not extend to Jesus of Nazareth. Oddly enough, the refusal of historians to consider Julius Caesar a god, despite being apotheosized by his contemporaries, is very rarely referred to as 'cutting Caesar down to size' or considered evidence of a 'draconian agenda.'

ATTACK OF THE ULTRACREPIDARIANS

The exchange of opinion that appeared in 2003 in the *Journal of Early Christian Studies* between Charles Hedrick, Guy Stroumsa—who has said, "the idea of a secret Gospel in the Alexandrian Church never really surprised me"[182]—and Bart Ehrman provided evidence that the authenticity of the "Secret" gospel of Mark was being taken seriously in some quarters, a revelation that provoked two ill-considered, pseudo-academic responses, Stephen Carlson's *The Gospel Hoax* and Peter Jeffery's *The Secret Gospel of Mark Unveiled*. Point-by-point interrogation of the arguments of these books continues to appear in various venues to which the reader will be referred. Nevertheless, the claims put forward must be at least briefly addressed, the flimsiness of their evidence notwithstanding.

It bears pointing out that *neither Stephen Carlson nor Peter Jeffery ever met Morton Smith* and that their reconstruction of his motives and personality is based entirely on secondhand reports and impressions gleaned from an overtly hostile, superficial, and polemically-motivated reading of some of his published work. However, mere lack of personal acquaintance has obviously not disqualified either author from imputing all sorts of ulterior motives and mental states to Smith. Despite their lack of access to Smith, his surviving notes on *Longer Mark*, or the manuscript that they claim to debunk, neither writer expresses his conclusions in terms of probabilities.

[182.] Stroumsa, *Morton Smith and Gershom Scholem*, xxi.

Indeed, both men write as if inspired, Carlson by hubris and Jeffery by malice. Carlson and Jeffery epitomize the *odium theologicum* that has blighted debate on *Longer Mark* from the very beginning.

In an exchange of opinion on the merits of Smith's discovery, Hedrick observed about the ad hominem attacks on Smith,

> Thirty years later, the reviews of Smith's books are almost embarrassing to read—not embarrassing to Smith, though I am sure they must have bothered him immensely at the time, but embarrassing to the academy. From my later perspective, the personal attacks on Smith were entirely unwarranted.[183]

Paul Foster, writing in 2008, expressed hope "that the debate will remain respectful and attentive to alternative points of view,"[184] while appearing to concede that the ship of comity had long since sailed. There will be more, substantially more, to say about the subject of character assassination as a strategy in the discussion that follows.

Smith's alleged homosexuality forms a major part of both Carlson's and Jeffery's attempted refutation of his work; a recent book by Stroumsa comments as follows on Smith's personal reticence: "Smith consistently shunned disclosure of his personal life…Smith's homosexuality was widely speculated upon in the American academic community."[185]

[183.] Hedrick, *Journal of Early Christian Studies* 11 (2003): 136.

[184.] Foster, *The Non-Canonical Gospels*, 181.

[185.] Stroumsa, *Morton Smith and Gershom Scholem*, xii, xiv, footnote 17.

Hershel Shanks also notes, "Smith's suspected (but unproven) homosexuality is another whispered and sometimes explicitly alleged motive [for forgery]."[186] Smith's personal correspondence was destroyed after his death, so as far as his sexual orientation is concerned it appears that Carlson and Jeffery have advanced their personal attacks against his character on the basis of rumor, faculty lounge speculation and malicious innuendo.

Lest my own position on the matter remain in any way unclear, let me say that I regard homosexual orientation as a normal and relatively common psychological variant and that any attempt to use sexual orientation as an accusation that impugns another's credibility or motives says nothing good about the rationality or professional ethics of the accuser. In any case, since it is considered routine for honest scholars to source their information, I fully expect that Carlson and Jeffery plan to produce their sources of information about Smith's private life at some prestigious academic conference that is soon to be announced.

Carlson's *Hoax*

Mark Goodacre and Larry Hurtado, timbrels ajangle, announced the victorious arrival of Carlson's book with breathless cover blurbs that suggested to the unwary that its author, a lawyer by trade, had made an epic scholarly

---

[186.] Shanks, *Biblical Archaeology Review*, November/December, 2009, 50.

breakthrough. Instead, the reader of *The Gospel Hoax*[187] is confronted by a tendentious daisy chain of microarguments that forcibly reminded me of Kierkegaard's complaint about being trampled by geese, and it is possible that some scholars who initially celebrated Carlson's book are, like Jephthah's daughter, feeling a little burned by subsequent developments.

Carlson's effort was poisoned from the outset by his prejudice, openly announced in the preface: "Now that I knew what to look for and where to look for it, all I had to do was find it."[188] His precious procedural *naïveté* on record, Carlson accomplished in a trice the goal he set for himself. It is, of course, axiomatic in Jesus Studies, as in every other discipline, that *a priori* conclusions are routinely confirmed to the complete satisfaction of those yearning for said conclusions. That Carlson's chorus line of supporters failed to notice this speaks directly to their credibility, to say nothing of their credulity.

Much of Carlson's evidence for forgery hinges on handwriting analysis of the Clement letter. The validity of handwriting analysis, or "forensic document verification" to use the approved term, has been questioned, but for the sake of argument I will stipulate that the procedure is reliable in expert hands. The American Board of Forensic Document Examiners recommends a baccalaureate degree and two years of "apprenticeship in a recognized forensic laboratory"[189] as

---

[187] Carlson, *The Gospel Hoax: Morton Smith's Invention of Secret Mark*, 2005, Baylor University Press.
[188] Ibid, xviii.
[189] www.abfde.org

the minimum qualifications for a document examiner. As a lawyer, I would suppose that Mr. Carlson was aware that those are *the minimum qualifications*. However, Carlson, to the best of my knowledge, had no formal training in either the field of paleography or in document verification, had never published in either field prior to writing his *Hoax*, nor was his opinion on the handwriting of the Clement letter vetted by a panel of disinterested experts on Greek script.

To this objection I must add another, even more blatantly obvious to anyone except his academic coreligionists: Carlson, working from reproductions of questionable quality, *claimed to know the document in question was a forgery without ever having seen the document*. In his summary of the circumstances of Smith's discovery, Ehrman noted that forgeries have been "uncovered by a careful analysis of the actual physical specimen."[190] Carlson never saw "the actual physical specimen" in question before claiming that Morton Smith, a scholar who expertise exceeded Carlson's own by at least several orders of magnitude, had committed fraud.[191] In common parlance this is known as "getting ahead of the evidence," not that that appears to have occurred to any of his fans.

The inadequacy of this amateur exercise has been thoroughly

---

[190] Ehrman, *Lost Christianities*, 85.

[191] A point made by Brown: "The techniques that Carlson uses for detecting forgery are intended for use on original documents rather than photographs." (*The Expository Times* 117 (2005): 145). However, the material Carlson used was *not* photographic, but halftone reproductions of photographs.

exposed by Scott Brown.[192] A close reading of his evidence for forgery reveals that Carlson negates much of his own argument. The features attributed to forgery can also occur due "to the writer's age, fatigue, stress level, or other causes for loss of fine motor control."[193] To which anyone might add yet other factors such as supporting a book on an unsteady surface while writing hurriedly. Shanks adds yet another: "The monk who wrote out the text was not simply writing out his own thoughts, but was copying another manuscript, which may account for the 'forger's tremor' and other characteristics of forgery that Carlson claims to detect."[194] Smith, who studied the complex cursive handwriting of the letter, including the many ligatures employed, noted the "small size of the letters together with the rapidity at which they were evidently written…"[195] It should emphasized that *Smith sought out the opinions of experts on Greek script*; he acknowledged Angelou and Dimaras (Greek National Foundation), Delatte (University of Liège), Kournoutos (Ministry of Education), Manousakas (Archives of the Academy of Athens), Nock (Harvard University), Richard (Institut de Recherche et d'Histoire des Textes), Scouvaras (Gymnasium of Volos), Soulis (Dumbarton Oaks Library) and Topping (University of Cincinnati).[196]

[192.] Brown, "Factualizing the Folklore: Stephen Carlson's Case Against Morton Smith," *Harvard Theological Review* 99 (2006): 291-327.
[193.] Carlson, *Gospel Hoax*, 26.
[194.] Shanks, *Biblical Archaeology Review*, November/December, 2009, 61.
[195.] Smith, *Clement of Alexandria*, 2.
[196.] Ibid, 1.

The claim of forgery based on Carlson's handwringing analysis has been definitively and decisively overturned by Roger Viklund's inspection of the photographic evidence. Working from color photos with higher resolution than the black and white reproductions used by Carlson, Viklund examined each of Carlson's claims in detail and failed to substantiate his conclusions.[197]

> All of these "signs" which Carlson spotted were not in the writing but an effect of the line screen that was used when the images were printed in Morton Smith's book. If Carlson had consulted the original photos instead of the printed copies, he would not have found those signs.[198]

More recently Viklund and Timo Paananen have published their findings in *Vigiliae Christianae*, concluding that the handwriting analysis argument in *The Gospel Hoax* "can be finally laid to rest."[199] Following a recent symposium on *Longer Mark*, Burke concluded,

> ...[Carlson's handwriting analysis] was based on examination of inadequate halftone photographs, its endorsement by a professional document examiner was misrepresented,[200] and the "clue" to the text's

---

[197.] Viklund, http://www.jesusgranskad.se/theodore.htm.

[198.] Viklund, http://rogerviklund.wordpress.com/category/scott-g-brown

[199.] Viklund & Paananen, *Vigiliae Christianae* 67 (2013), 247.

[200.] The document examiner, Julie Edison, who was 'consulted' by Carlson did not, in fact, express any opinion about who wrote

authorship in the signature of "M. Madiotes" in manuscript 22 appears to be baseless. If there is any agreement among the scholars of the symposium it is that these arguments are no longer useful, for aside from a brief mention in Evan's paper, Carlson's analysis was all but ignored even by supporters of forgery.[201]

Nevertheless, the implications of Viklund and Paananen's efforts, which have negated Carlson's handwriting claims, have yet to penetrate some corners of academia—Viklund and Paananen are airily dismissed by Pierluigi Piovanelli as "some Scandinavian bloggers."[202] However, Dr. Piovanelli's brushoff has inadvertently exposed a fundamental problem: while tenured professors from university departments were being uncritically suckered by Carlson's handwriting imposture, bloggers from the margins of the academy were actually testing his claims against the evidence, a situation that, once exposed, was unlikely to inspire confidence in the integrity of the academy.

Years after Carlson's book was received with joyful acclaim and his conclusions imprudently accepted as foregone by some New Testament scholars, the editors of *Biblical Archaeology Review*, essentially retracing the footsteps of Morton Smith, engaged a real handwriting expert, Venetia

---

the Clement letter and has "a limited knowledge of the Greek alphabet." (Brown & Pantuck, *Ancient Gospel or Modern Forgery?*, 123.)

[201.] Burke, Ibid, 26.
[202.] Piovanelli, Ibid, 160.

Anastasopoulou, whose extensive credentials appear to be in order. Anastasopoulou compared Smith's Greek hand with the script of the letter to Theodore and rendered an opinion on Smith's ability to forge the complex cursive script of the Clement letter. After making a thorough comparison of the script of the letter and Smith's visibly less fluent handwritten Greek, Anastasopoulou concluded in part,

> Moreover, the level of [Smith's] ability concerning his Greek language handwriting characteristics is like that of young school children who have not started to use writing in a practical way expressing thoughts and ideas. Thus Morton Smith could possibly imitate a copy booked, immature and impersonal writing, but it would be unlikely for him to imitate writing with high-level rhythm. With the same thinking, he could imitate a high-level writing in English rather than a copy booked, immature and impersonal English writing.[203]

In short, Anastasopoulou could find no evidence to suggest that Smith had the ability to forge a 17th century cursive script.

A second expert on Greek script, Agamemnon Tselikas, came to the exact opposite conclusion (expressed in a mixture of English and Yodaese):

> The history of the text of St. Clement offers no evidence of an earlier copy of the letter. In none of

---

[203.] Anastasopoulou, http://www.bib-arch.org/pdf/secret-mark-analysis. Pdf.

the manuscripts that transmit the Clement's texts the letter is contained. So this letter is the only attributed to Clement...I think that is impossible for someone to write this text inside the monastery since 1923... Most convincing is that the edition of Ignatius with the letter already written by Morton Smith or by someone else was placed in the library by Morton Smith himself...My conclusion is that the letter is product of forgery and all the evidence suggest that the forger can not be other person than Morton Smith or some other person under his orders..."[204]

Detailed critiques of Tselikas' response that cast doubt on his conclusions have, of course, appeared,[205] as well as counter-arguments from Tselikas, who characterized his critics as "parasites of real and true science."[206] However, very little of Tselikas' speculative reconstruction of Smith's alleged forgery scheme counts as "science." Tselikas has offered no "formal critical argument"[207] for his conclusion about handwriting, but has rather expanded the conspiracy hypothesis to include a shadowy collaborator engaged by Smith to produce the

---

[204.] Tselikas, *Ancient Gospel or Modern Forgery?*, 142-144.

[205.] Pantuck, "Response to Agamemnon Tselikas on Morton Smith and the Manscripts from Cephalonia," http://www.biblicalarchaeology.org/ uncategorized/allan-j-pantuck-response-to-tselikas-handwriting-analysis/. See particularly Viklund's post (rogerviklund.wordpress.com/category/allen-j-pantuck/).

[206.] http://www.biblicalarchaeology.org/uncategorized/agamemnon-tseli-kas-response-to-allan-j-pantuck/

[207.] Hedrick, *Ancient Gospel or Modern Forgery?*, 37.

cursive script that Smith himself was incapable of writing. Smith supposedly then smuggled the book into the library and "discovered" it. Who such an unindicted co-conspirator may have been, where and how Smith may have met such a person, and what motive might have induced this mysterious entity to cooperate in fraud are left to the imagination.

As any American alive since the assassination of John F. Kennedy can attest, there is no "off" switch to conspiracy theory. Common sense, probability, and contradictory evidence almost never defeat conspiratorial thinking, which simply broadens the scope of the conspiracy to "explain" the countervailing evidence. Conspiracy theorists can reject what is known, what is likely, and what is coherent by concocting a story of the unknown, the unlikely, and the incoherent, but nevertheless produce a narrative that cannot ultimately be disconfirmed, a tactic sometimes referred to as "Russell's Teapot." It is significant that appeal to nonfalsifiable claims is the hallmark of fake science, theology, and bullshit in general. Conspiracy as a response to Smith's find is not a new ploy. Smith's early detractors could find no evidence whatsoever that tended to confirm the letter's authenticity—everything that seemed to confirm Smith's discovery was proof of forgery and every inconsistency also proof of forgery. Smith, aware of the claim that inconsistencies had been planted in the letter because "they were things a forger would not do," responded, "With such a theory you can't lose. The things that fit your thesis fit; the things that don't also fit…When a theory must be defended by such hypotheses it is indefensible."[208]

[208.] Smith, *Catholic Biblical Quarterly* 38 (1976): 197.

Scott Brown has raised the same objection to Carlson's dishonest methodology. "Any behavior that could attest to Smith's integrity is ascribed to deception, whereas any behavior that could be construed as suspicious is deemed incriminating. A theory of motive that can explain any behavior and its opposite, however, has nothing to recommend it. Useful theories must be refutable in principle, which means they must have testable implications."[209]

Others, much closer to the sources of this controversy than I, have remarked on Carlson's inept methodology. "The author's legal training and his lack of philological acumen clearly show throughout the [*Gospel Hoax*]."[210] The strength of the evidence for forgery is directly proportional to one's eagerness to see it. Some people see images of Jesus on toasted bread, in clouds, or on tree bark, but I must humbly confess to never have received a similar pareidolic epiphany of the Father, Son, or Holy Toast. It bears repeating that *Smith submitted photos of the letter to experts on Greek handwriting* who placed the handwriting around 1750,[211] a verdict that would seem to be substantiated.

Although Carlson claimed to have consulted a qualified document examiner, Julie C. Edison, who vouched for his work, it turns out that Ms. Edison is unable to read Greek, met with Carlson for only a few hours during which they examined inadequate halftone reproductions, and has since

---

[209] Brown, *Journal of Biblical Literature* 125 (2006): 374.

[210] Stroumsa, *Morton Smith and Gershom Scholem*, xiv, footnote 18.

[211] Smith, *Clement of Alexandria*, 1.

prudently disavowed "having expressed an opinion on the manuscript's authenticity."[212]

These observations lead me another of Carlson's claims, namely that the overweening Smith planted references to himself within the Clement letter to tweak the noses of his fellow academics. Only a very clever person indeed would be able to spot these hidden signatures and Carlson imagines himself to be that very person, a delusion that may account for the smirking, self-congratulatory tone of his book.

The fatuity of this project culminates in the identification of a passing mention of salt—"even the salt loses its flavor"[213]—as a reference to Morton Smith (Morton Smith = Morton's Salt, get it? Snigger, snigger). A lengthy critique of this bizarre argument has been written by Kyle Smith of Duke University, who concludes, "there is little reason to dismiss *Theodore*'s use of the salt parable as un-Clementine. More to the point, there is no reason at all to believe Carlson's argument that Theodore's reference to salt is anachronistic. Salt could be (and was) both mixed and adulterated in antiquity, and to suggest that salt could not be mixed unless it is free-flowing salt with anti-caking agents added to it is belied by numerous ancient and modern references. In sum, it is now clear that Carlson was overly hasty. He spotted a reference to salt and, since he was probing the text for clues to its inauthenticity, jumped to make a connection between Morton Smith and

---

[212.] Brown & Pantuck,
http://salainenevankelista.blogspot.com/2010/-04/stephen-carlson-questionable.html.

[213.] Compare the text of the letter, page 15.

Morton's Salt...by my reckoning, Carlson is down 0-1."[214] Brown has also addressed Carlson's fantasy about the salt metaphor: "Carlson's highly unorthodox approach to interrogating the texts has elicited another false confession."[215] Hershel Shanks adds, "In antiquity salt was regularly mixed with other substances."[216]

As an additional proof of the hoax hypothesis—although he has claimed that Smith produced one of the 20th century's greatest fakes, Carlson is oddly squeamish about the word "forgery"—Carlson alleges that Smith essentially 'signed' his falsification with the name "M. Madiotes" (Μαδιοτης) on a Mar Saba document (MS no. 22)—*another document Carlson has never actually seen*—that is separate from the Clement letter.[217] This whimsical line of attack evidently suggested itself to him because the Greek μαδαρος means "bald" and Smith was bald. Noting the "element of the preposterous" in Carlson's claim, Edward Smith wondered "how many of those who accepted Carlson's position on this really stopped to ponder how likely

---

[214.] Smith, "Mixed with Inventions: Salt and Metaphor in Secret Mark," available on Wieland Willker's New Testament homepage (www.user.-uni-bremen.de/-wie/Secret/SecMark). For the record it should be noted that Kyle Smith is not convinced that the Clement letter or gospel fragments are genuine.

[215.] Brown, *Harvard Theological Review* 99 (2006): 313.

[216.] Shanks, "Restoring a Dead Scholar's Reputation," *Biblical Archaeology Review*, November/December, 2009, 60.

[217.] Carlson, *Gospel Hoax*, 42-44.

anyone would be to describe himself as either bald or a swindler."[218]

In a recently published refutation of this flight of fancy, which includes a reexamination of Smith's notes and photographic material in the archives of the Jewish Theological Seminary in New York, Pantuck and Brown concluded, "this evidence indicates that Carlson's 'Madiotes' theory is incorrect in all of its aspects" and noted the danger of working with materials "three steps removed from the original."[219]

Naturally Carlson does not fail to make an issue of Smith's sexuality. It may be fairly asked if this is part of the reason his book was published by Baylor University Press, the publishing arm of the notoriously homophobic Baylor University, the school that found a Starbucks coffee cup with a quotation from gay author Armistead Maupin[220] so threatening to its identity that its administration had the cups removed. I supply this bit of background lest the unsuspecting reader assume that Baylor University, the world's largest Baptist school, located in the heart of Texas, North America's largest free range insane asylum, represents a source of reasoned inquiry. The intellectual universe of Baylor University—"Westboro Lite"—is one of the outer planets of the Bible Belt and closely reflects both denominational prejudice and hostility to

---

[218] Smith, *The Temple Sleep of the Rich Young Ruler*, 248.

[219] Pantuck & Brown, *Journal for the Study of the Historical Jesus*, 6 (2008): 112, 114.

[220] Maupin, author of the *Tales of the City* novels, is an American military veteran who once worked for Senator Jesse Helms.

contrary opinion.[221] The press of a jumped up Bible college is a shaky platform from which to launch attacks on a distinguished scholar's motives.

It is quite ironic that Carlson castigated Smith for cluttering his evidence with "historically worthless testimonia,"[222] which he has simply decreed to have no relevance to the question of authenticity, but uses up 23 pages (by my count) of his slender book to expatiate on such varied subjects as faked artifacts, *Piltdown Man*, Pfaff's forgery of Irenaeus, the Coleman-Norton agraphon, and how CBS supposedly got its story wrong about George W. Bush's personal exit strategy from the Vietnam War, all of which are presumed to have some unrecognized bearing on the authenticity of the Clement letter. On cross-examination, Carlson's book fails in each and every particular argument. In his summary of Carlson's case, *il etait une fois* when Piovanelli said, "Pourtant, en dépit de l'acumulation de toutes ces présomptions de culpabilité, le point crucial est de savoir, non pas si Smith a effectivement agi de la sorte (car reste, à notre avis, en l'absence de toute prevue matérielle, quasiment impossible à démontrer), mais s'il est envisageable qu'un savant de sa carrure se soit donné la peine de faire tout ceci pour des raisons aussi puériles."[223]

It is tempting to theorize that Carlson wrote his book to see

---

[221.] The interested reader is referred to Brown's "The Question of Motive in the Case Against Morton Smith," *The Journal of Biblical Literature* 125 (2006): 351, ff.

[222.] Carlson, *Gospel Hoax*, 88.

[223.] Piovanelli, *Revue Biblique* 114 (2007): 245.

how scholars would react to a fake refutation of a real discovery. In any event, Carlson's attempt to plant incriminating evidence to malign Morton Smith has failed, but it is probably too much to hope that the doyens of the conservative Jesus Studies field, who have until now demonstrated a nearly infinite capacity for being hornswoggled, might succumb to *textual evidence*, the generally accepted basis for exegesis. Edward R. Smith, himself a lawyer with an interest in "Secret" Mark, ably summarized Carlson's approach: "unlike a detective, who starts with a crime scene, identifies objective clues amid the evidence, and then follows them back to a suspect, Carlson starts with the suspect, finds features in the evidence that could, with research and ingenuity, be construed as clues left behind by that suspect, and then uses these clues as evidence for a crime scene," a procedure Smith aptly describes as an "inversion of the scientific method."[224]

Peter Jeffery uncorked

If Stephen Carlson's book is tendentious and weak, it is a monument to objectivity compared to the academic quackery of Peter Jeffery, a musicologist. Jeffery's book, *The Secret Gospel of Mark Unveiled: Imagined Rituals of Sex, Death, and Madness in a Biblical Forgery*, published with the financial assistance of the Kingsley Trust Association, the public face of the Scroll and Key Society, one of Yale's several "secret" societies, is the *Worlds in Collision* of New Testament studies. Although *Unveiled* pretends to eschew "armchair

---

[224.] Smith, *The Temple Sleep of the Rich Young Ruler*, 249.

psychoanalysis dressed up as objective scholarship,"[225] the book fairly oozes it. Smith's recollection of his discovery is described in psychiatric terms like "extreme mood swings and bouts of amnesia"[226] and "dissociative episodes."[227] These *medical diagnoses* come, not from a physician who treated Smith, but from a music teacher who never met the subject of his armchair psychoanalysis.

Jeffery's prose is humorless, flatulent and pompous, a condescending drone punctuated by tidbits of self-righteous twaddle such as this gem: "And I pray for the late Morton Smith—may God rest his anguished soul."[228] If there is anything on which Peter Jeffery, a Benedictine oblate, is less of an authority than *Longer Mark* it is undoubtedly the state of Morton Smith's soul.

Jeffery bases his arguments on two assumptions: first, that the linen garment worn by the youth mentioned in *Longer Mark* is evidence of a baptismal ritual, and second, that Smith fabricated the Clement letter to discredit Christianity by making Jesus homosexual. In both cases, he claims to find anachronisms that disprove the authenticity of the letter.

It may be conceded that Smith, like millions of other people, had an ax to grind with Christianity, but his claims regarding a sexualized Jesus must be examined in the context of his total

---

[225.] Jeffery, *The Secret Gospel of Mark Unveiled*, 35.
[226.] Ibid, 18.
[227.] Ibid, 29.
[228.] Ibid, ix.

scholarly output, a precaution rarely taken,[229] possibly relevant gospel passages that Jeffery predictably ignores, and the evidence of early critics and "heresiologists."[230] Many scholars have pointed to evidence of Jesus' prickly family relationships as well as indications of sexual ambiguity and erotic imagery, but Professor Jeffery appears queerly unaware of such controversies. *Queerly* in that Jeffery speculates endlessly about the sexuality of confirmed bachelor Morton Smith, but makes no comment at all about the confirmed bachelor Jesus of Nazareth.

In the first place, Jeffery assumes the validity of Smith's belief that the gospel fragments reflect a baptismal initiation rite, effectively viewing the Clement letter through the prism of Smith's interpretation of it—"Rather than starting with the text itself and using established procedures for determining its meaning, most scholars have been starting with an assumption or hypothesis about what the meaning *might* be."[231] Indeed, Jeffery's stated strategy is to *avoid* textual analysis: "Almost all the discussion has been focused on the Secret Gospel and its relationship to canonical Mark, perhaps the very place a forger (if there was a forger) wanted us to look…" Instead, Professor Jeffery prefers to move "erudite discussion,"[232] in which he imagines himself to be a participant, to the purely speculative realm, perhaps the very place an academic fraudster (if there is a fraudster) wants us

---

[229.] Brown, *Journal of Biblical Literature* 125 (2006): 354-373.
[230.] See Conner, *Magic in Christianity*, 22-40.
[231.] Brown, *The Fourth R*, 25/6, 5.
[232.] Jeffery, *The Secret Gospel of Mark Unveiled*, 42.

to look. "Yet [*Longer Mark* and its relationship to canonical Mark] is really the primary, if not the only, area of relevance."[233]

Starting from Smith's interpretation, Jeffery argues that such a reading of the evidence reflects the modern Anglican liturgy with which Smith was most familiar and is therefore anachronistic. In an attempt to prove this argument, he drags his victims through a soporific swamp of ecclesiastical trivia, including two excruciating chapters on liturgiology and Alexandrine lectionaries, after which he observes, "The more enmeshed we get in the complexities of early liturgical history, the harder it is to believe that we will eventually find traces of the Secret Gospel," a conclusion the moribund reader has doubtless reached many pages past, and then adds, in a rare flash of lucidity, "fortunately we do not need to."[234] Shanks remarks of Jeffery's style, a masterpiece of Jesuitical obfuscation, "some of his arguments are so dense and arcane that no ordinary human being can follow them to refute them."[235]

Like nearly all writers who regard the letter as a forgery, Jeffery blindly follows Smith's interpretation of his find, particularly the letter's reference to the mysteries which Smith —mistakenly in my opinion—understood as an allusion to baptism. In fact, Clement very rarely refers to baptism as a

---

[233.] Smith, *The Temple Sleep of the Rich Young Ruler*, 215.
[234.] Ibid, 91.
[235.] Shanks, *Ancient Gospel or Modern Forgery?*, 136.

mystery,[236] but the point I wish to make is that Jeffery merely starts where Smith left off. Rather than provisionally assume that the letter might be authentic and perform his own textual —as opposed to sexual—analysis of the letter 'from the ground up,' he simply gathered up Smith's conclusions, belying his claim—"begin with the document"[237]—that his evaluation of the evidence began with the Clement letter.

That such a textual analysis might have occurred presumes that Jeffery had the desire or capacity to perform it in the first place, a presumption for which his book supplies no evidence. In any event, if the "greater mysteries" referred instead to a progressive revelation of hidden knowledge and not to baptism, then the whole structure of his argument on baptismal liturgy collapses in a heap. It is unmentioned and perhaps unknown by Jeffery that the idea that the "greater mysteries" referred to baptism was not Smith's, but was proposed to him by a professor of church history, Cyril Richardson. Smith regarded the suggestion as "a brilliant analysis"[238] and subsequently abandoned the notion that the mysteries involved increasing gnosis.

It bears repeating that *the Clement letter says absolutely nothing*

[236.] Brown, Review of Biblical Literature 09/2007 (www.bookreviews. Org/pdf/5627_5944.pdf). This is the most thorough refutation of Jeffery to date. See particularly Brown's "Behind the Seven Veils, I: The Gnostic Life Setting of the Mystic Gospel of Mark," *Ancient Gospel or Modern Forgery?*, 247-283.

[237.] Jeffery, *The Secret Gospel of Mark Unveiled*, 246.

[238.] Smith, *The Secret Gospel*, 61.

about baptism nor does Jeffery address the question of why baptism, a rite administered to *all* Christians, would qualify as a *greater* mystery available only to the elect. That the greater mysteries pertained to baptism and that the linen cloth was a baptismal garment were inferred by Smith, but there is no support for this inference in the letter to Theodore or in the gospels, where the linen sheet is repeatedly linked to preparation for burial,[239] not baptism. A more convincing alternative scenario, which Jeffery completely ignores, has been proposed and will be discussed in detail in a later section. I am almost convinced that Jesus foresaw Jeffery's book when he said, "For those outside, everything happens in parables."[240]

Against Smith's interpretation of the mysteries as baptism, one might simply point to the obvious: *the gospels have no baptism-by-Jesus stories to tell*, an amazing omission given that baptism by the highest authority figure in Christianity might have served to clearly establish an apostolic chain of command—baptism by an apostle was thought to confer exceptional status, although it appears not to have been the focus of the earliest missionaries. Paul, after all, declared, "Christ did not send me to baptize."[241] Jesus is recorded as giving his disciples power over spirits,[242] a commission to preach the coming end,[243] and authority to bind earthly things

---

[239] Matthew 27:59, Mark 15:46, Luke 28:53.
[240] Mark 4:11.
[241] 1 Corinthians 1:13-17.
[242] Mark 6:7.
[243] Matthew 10:7.

with heavenly consequences,[244] *but did not baptize anyone.*[245] Surely if Jesus had baptized disciples such an event would be recalled as significant by some strand of the early tradition, but the gospels do not record the baptism of any of the apostles, or, insofar as I am aware, of any key figure other than Jesus. The significance of the linen sheet lies somewhere other than a baptismal ritual.

If Smith misinterpreted the letter to Theodore, it would strongly imply that the letter was genuine, not a forgery. That a forger would misapprehend a work of his own imagination is nearly absurd—unless perhaps the forger was Peter Jeffery. But that a person who discovered an ancient document might fail to completely grasp its significance is not only understandable, it is likely. Smith's failure in that regard not only tends to exonerate him, it works to establish the authenticity of the letter. Smith's discovery then becomes much like any other such event: a scholar stumbles upon a document from the distant past, studies it, publishes his findings, some of which are later found to contain conclusions that are spot on and others that are mistaken. Further investigation and reflection corrects the mistakes. Ironically, Smith's detractors cannot follow this very ordinary process without taking Smith's baptismal interpretation at face value and so must accept his almost certainly flawed interpretation to attack his almost certainly genuine discovery. But that Smith's thinking about the letter underwent an expected progression is now confirmed by the recent release

---

[244] Matthew 18:18.
[245] John 4:2.

of his correspondence with his mentor and friend Gershom Scholem.

The second principle part of Jeffery's case against Smith concerns the homosexual narrative that Smith supposedly advanced to discredit Jesus. (The notion that Jesus' ethical teaching could be utterly overturned by a revelation of homosexuality reveals a peculiar mindset, but that is not our subject.) To prosecute his case against Smith, Jeffery dramatically "unveils" the rather ordinary conflicts of a conservative homosexual (?) minister living in the 1950's America of McCarthy and Hoover and like Carlson, Jeffery projects a series of gay sex-in-the-bushes stereotypes on a cardboard figure of Smith. It is this fixation on Smith's sexual orientation that most clearly exposes the boorish ineptitude of both writers—Smith's opaque inner life, about which neither Carlson or Jeffery can claim to know the slightest item of substance, is made the subject of caricature.

Jeffery has advanced his speculative reinvention of Smith's character on "unpublished anecdotes I have heard about him."[246] I have heard some unpublished anecdotes about Peter Jeffery that tend to confirm my impression of him, but I'll leave it at that. In the interests of intellectual honesty and full disclosure, Carlson and Jeffery should unveil their sources pertaining to Smith's personal life, but given the general dishonesty of the attacks on Smith, I suspect it is unlikely any such clarification will ever happen.

[246.] Jeffery, *The Secret Gospel of Mark Unveiled*, 243. "I never met Smith myself, after all…" (*Unveiled*, 236).

The Secret Gospel of Mark Unveiled is above all else a heavy-breathing rumination on homosex. Professor Jeffery can barely tear himself away from the topic; it is the theme of nearly half his book, a theme to which he returns with evident relish and compulsive fury. The underlying malice and distortion with which the whole matter is addressed finally seeps to the surface in this memorable quote: "the hunt is on for a 'gay gene,' which, if discovered, might have a greater impact on the abortion rate than on cultural attitudes toward homosexuality."[247] The professor's better-dead-than-queer sentiments are typical of that generation of aging Catholic altar boys janxy about the progression of legal parity for gays. Homosexuals might be legally married, ordained, or even one day perform the ultimate blasphemy—faith n' begorrah!—march in a Saint Paddy's Day parade. In his review of Jeffery's jihad, the historian William Harris, who knew Smith and was by his own admission not particularly fond of him, remarks on Jeffery's "vicious hostility" and notes, as have several others, that he "confuses the question of the authenticity of the text and the validity of Smith's interpretation of it."[248]

After a lengthy review of Jeffery's book, Brown concluded,

> Like the modern anachronisms pertaining to baptism, sexual humor, and homosexual culture that he "unveiled" by misreading the letter's Gospel excerpts in three incompatible ways, the violent depravity that Jeffery exposes is wholly the product of eisegesis. What could lead a person to imagine so much

---

[247] Ibid, 248.
[248] Harris, *Times Literary Supplement*, 5455, 10/19/2007, 23.

depravity and falsity in a non-canonical Gospel and the person who discovered it? That is the only question that this book leaves me pondering.[249]

I will confess, after some reflection on the matter, that Jeffery's masterpiece is simply the most bizarre thing in any category of literature that I have ever read. But the review of his work by J. Harold Ellens, a psychologist *and* theologian—which I suppose must qualify him as a practitioner of psychotheology—comes in a very close second. Ellens' paean to Jeffery begins, "This superbly packaged book, lovely to read, hold, fondle, smell, and contemplate as an aesthetic object…"[250] and rhapsodizes on from there, as insubstantial and inoffensive as a simple summer lay. Applying Jeffery's own idiosyncratic canons of interpretation to Ellens' review, one might conjecture that Dr. Ellens yearns to "hold, fondle, smell and contemplate" Dr. Jeffery's lovely "package."

If Peter Jeffery is anything, he is the acknowledged prince of sexual *double entendre*. Assuming that Smith was a pervert, Jeffery accordingly finds all manner of sexual jokes in the Clement letter, planted there by Smith to ridicule his fellow academics and heap contempt on the Christian religion. Jeffery characterizes Smith's book on *Longer Mark* as "the most grandiose and reticulated 'Fuck You' ever perpetrated in the long and vituperative history of scholarship."[251] Reimagined through his "prurient eyes,"[252] the woman whose

---

[249] Brown, *Review of Biblical Literature*, September 15, 2007, 1-47.
[250] Ellens, http://www.bookreview.org/pdf/5627_7785.pdf.
[251] Jeffery, *The Secret Gospel of Mark Unveiled*, 242.
[252] Ibid, 93.

brother had died "threw herself" (προσεκυνησε) before Jesus," an expression that Jeffery translates, "bent down to kiss" in a reference to oral sex. When Jesus enters the tomb to raise the *neaniskos* from the dead—"he stretched out his hand and raised him, holding his hand"—Jeffery detects another sexual allusion: "the word 'hand' can also be taken as a euphemism for another, more intimate body part."[253] In a recently published essay, Jeffery unveils more sexual innuendo—if anything, Jeffery's *nostalgie de la boue* has only worsened with age. Clement's comment that Mark prepared his textual expansion, "neither grudgingly nor carelessly" (ου φθονερως ουδ' απροφυλακτως) becomes in Jeffery's hand, undoubtedly calloused after so much sexual fantasizing, "neither jealously nor without a condom."[254] The term απροφυλακτος (aprophulaktos), *unforeseen, without precautions*, is thereby transformed into "without a prophylactic" by the text-deaf musicologist.

Professor Jeffery is a master at stating the obvious: "…most advocates of an ancient origin strongly resist reading the epistle [to Theodore] as one of Smith's writings." This axiom is followed by a round of question begging: "Those who try the hardest to understand [Smith] are consistently appalled…"[255] He then cites several examples of scholars who apparently strove to understand Smith but had serious reservations about his methodology. Speaking as one who has read much of his work and extensively referenced his

---

[253.] Ibid, 94.
[254.] Jeffery, *Ancient Gospel or Modern Forgery?*, 243.
[255.] Ibid, 214.

writings, I have on occasion been underwhelmed by Smith's argumentation but never appalled. There are obviously others, perhaps many others, who have read Smith's work closely and have not been "consistently appalled." Oblivious to fallacy, Jeffery continues, "Indeed, ruling out Smith's authorship [of the letter to Theodore, my note] *a priori*…actually sets up a circular argument from which there is no escape."[256] Indeed, ruling out *Clement's* authorship of the letter to Theodore *a priori* also sets up a circular argument from which there is no escape.

Jeffery slights the work of Meyer and Brown, passes over the work of Crossan, Koester and Dart, and in general seems uninterested in or acquainted with much of the literature on *Longer Mark*, and at no point gives any hint that he might be competent to evaluate it in the first place. This verdict is supported by his parroting of Bruce's claim that the gospel fragments are "a cento of words and phrases from the canonical gospels and other ancient writings,"[257] an allegation that enjoys scant currency because it has so little to recommend it. However, he has at least opened *Clement of Alexandria*, a work derided as,

> …a relentless succession of stray facts, held together by quasi-facts, propped up by non-facts, painstakingly built up, like papier-mâché, into something that looks like a deliberate parody of scholarship itself, drumming the glassy-eyed reader into submission like some hypnotic ritual hymn. It is as if we have

---
[256.] Ibid, 215.
[257.] *The Secret Gospel of Mark Unveiled*, 91.

ascended to a lawless paradise in which all principles of interpretation and reasoning have been suspended, where almost anything can prove almost anything.[258]

Which particular facts in *Clement of Alexandria* are "stray," which "quasi" and which are "non" Jeffery must leave to our lawless imagination. Eyer noted the criticism that Smith used "too much documentation as a ploy to confuse the reader,"[259] an objection that makes the befuddlement of the critic the fault of Smith's detailed argument. Like Carlson, Jeffery presumes to have dismissed a solid work of textual analysis with rhetorical afflatus.

However, when it comes to parodies of scholarship, the suspension of reason and principles of interpretation—to say nothing of hypnotic ritual hymns—Jeffery is clearly in his element. In fact, his argumentation is so farfetched as to be nearly incomprehensible. His book even contains a chapter on homosexuality in British boys' schools, "Uranian Venus: Homoerotic Subcultures in English Universities."[260] That the subject of schoolboy sodomy, once universally assumed to have no bearing on the authentication of ancient gospels, could be adduced as evidence was utterly unsuspected before Kapellmeister Jeffery published.

The *Secret Gospel of Mark Unveiled* is a veritable shelter for stray facts; Jeffery cites all manner of authority figures in

---

[258] Ibid, 120.

[259] Eyer, *Alexandria: The Journal for the Western Cosmological Traditions* 3 (1995), 107.

[260] Jeffery, *The Secret Gospel of Mark Unveiled*, 213-225.

support of his sexual thesis, Walter Pater,[261] Michelangelo,[262] Havelock Ellis,[263] George Frederick Handel,[264] Christopher Marlowe,[265] E.M. Forster,[266] and, of course, Oscar Wilde, the ultimate homosexual whipping boy, who inevitably functioned as a model for Smith, as he supposedly does for homosexuals generally, because apparently all Catholics know how much all inverts revere Oscar Wilde.[267]

As anyone who wishes might very easily learn, the 1950's America to which Smith returned after studying in Israel was a racially segregated society riven by reactionary politics, a status still very much in force in America's unreconstructed neo-Confederacy where Christian "segregation academies," supported by taxpayers, are still quite common.

No two figures became more emblematic of the era's culture of paranoia and intimidation than Joseph McCarthy and Roy Cohn. In 1952, the publisher of the tabloid *Las Vegas Sun*, Hank Greenspun, accused McCarthy, "a bachelor of 43 years,"[268] of being a closeted homosexual and rather than suing Greenspun for libel and risk testifying under oath about his sexual proclivities, McCarthy opted to marry Jean Kear, one of his office staff, in 1953. McCarthy, who had been

---

[261.] Ibid, 215-218.
[262.] Ibid, 215, 217-218.
[263.] Ibid, 214.
[264.] Ibid, 214, 234.
[265.] Ibid, 223-224.
[266.] Ibid, 214, 220.
[267.] Ibid, 231-234.
[268.] Greenspun, *Las Vegas Sun*, October 25, 1952.

elected with enthusiastic Catholic support, died of hepatitis at Bethesda Naval Hospital in 1957 at the age of 48. Although McCarthy's liver failure is generally attributed to alcoholism, it bears mention that hepatitis can also be sexually transmitted. As is well known, Cohn, a closeted homosexual, was disbarred from the practice of law due to repeated fraud, and died of AIDS in 1986.

During the decades Smith spent establishing his academic bona fides and moving up the career ladder, Republicans regularly campaigned on getting the "lavender lads," thought to represent a national security risk, out of government positions, particularly in the Department of State. Homosexuals had more to fear than the malice of backstabbing colleagues, however. Particularly following the publication of von Kraft-Ebing's *Psychopathia Sexualis* (1894), homosexuals or "urnings," were described as inferior, degenerate *Untermenschen* and could be involuntarily committed and sterilized. At one point, 32 states in America had such laws based on "eugenics" and it is now widely known that those laws were applied with particular rigor to racial minorities and homosexual men and women. In fact, it was not only sadistic Nazi doctors who were publicly endorsing "castration for the cure of homosexuality in the male."[269]

In 1952, the British genius, Alan Turing, who invented the device used to decipher German code and thus anticipate the movement of German U boats during the Battle of the Atlantic—saving the lives of thousands of Allied sailors—

---

[269] *British Medical Journal* 1 (April 6, 1946): 551.

agreed to chemical castration to avoid imprisonment after being convicted of homosexuality under the same law used to prosecute Oscar Wilde in 1895. In 1954, Turing committed suicide. In America, in 1953, President Eisenhower signed Executive Order 10450 under which "sexual perverts" were fired from federal jobs; before 1962, sodomy was a felony in every American state.

Walter J. Freeman, who began performing lobotomy in 1936, traveled to 23 American states—"head hunting" as he jokingly called it—in his "lobotomobile," eventually performing his surgical driveby on at least 3,439 victims. Wearing neither mask or gloves, Freeman peeled back the upper eyelid, positioned a metal pick above the eyeball, hammered it into the cranium through the bone of the eye socket, and moved it back and forth, severing neural connections between the frontal lobes and the rest of the brain. The operation became common; it was performed after 1945 on as many as 2000 military veterans suffering from "shell shock;"[270] Freeman performed this ghoulish procedure on 19 children less than 18 years of age, in one case committing the atrocity on a child of four. He lobotomized one victim, a twelve-year-old boy, who had been diagnosed with "day-dreaming." Needless to say, lobotomy was also used on the 'morally insane,' particularly homosexuals.[271]

In mental hospitals where Freeman and others did lobotomies, as many as 30 to 40% of victims are thought to

---

[270.] http://projects.wsj.com/lobotomyfiles/?ch=two.
[271.] http://www.apa.org/monitor/2011/02/myth-buster.aspx.

have been homosexuals.[272] Around 15% of lobotomy victims died as a result and others lapsed into a vegetative state. Freeman, who described his psychic murder as "surgically induced childhood," was finally stopped from his own moral insanity in 1976 after a victim, whom he had similarly assaulted on two previous occasions, died of cerebral hemorrhage.

The Soviet Union outlawed lobotomy in 1950 on humanitarian grounds, and Germany and Japan, whose war atrocities in the 1930's and 1940's were unprecedented, followed suit a few years later. In America, however, lobotomy continued until the advent of the drug chlorpromazine, originally marketed as a "chemical lobotomy." The United States Congress eventually voted for the formation of a regulatory body, the National Committee for the Protection of Human Subjects of Biomedical and Behavioral Research in 1977, only eight years before Smith finally retired.

For gays in the America in which Smith spent nearly all of his life an arrest for merely being in a bar and having one's name published in a newspaper as a consequence were nearly the least of one's worries. Smith's America was not one in which 19th century aesthetes or upper crust Athenians well into their cups debated the merits of *paiderastia*. It was a country where racial and sexual minorities were systematically brutalized under the complacent and complicit gaze of medical, state, and *religious* authorities. The imagined "commonplaces of

---

[272.] http://www.davidmixner.com/2010/07/lgbt-history-the-decade-of-lobotomies-castration-and-institutions.html

[Smith's] post-Uranian construction of sexuality"[273] are the flaccid projections of Peter Jeffery, an authority on religious chanting, who has spun out a despicable airy-fairy, artsy-fartsy, obscenely ignorant fantasy in the form of a contemptible book that in no way reflects the social reality for homosexual men and women of Smith's era.

Which leads me at last to this question: what evidence do Carlson and Jeffery actually have? They certainly have no confession from Smith, nor does either have an original document professionally examined. They do, however, have clear presupposition of guilt, arguments based on homophobia, fideism, rumor and conjecture, hastily drawn conclusions based on amateur sleuthing and fanciful arguments that I, among others, believe are an embarrassment to the academy. Unsurprisingly, they have managed quite easily to rationalize the suspicions of some who already harbored hostility to Smith and his interpretation of the Clement letter. Carlson has done what any lawyer does: cast doubt on one explanation of the evidence while proposing another that coincides with the personal sensibilities and prejudices of his audience. An authority here and there has changed sides as a result, but it is hard to name a conspiracy theory that has failed to attract a few high profile supporters.

Any lessons learned?

The four-decade-old controversy about *Longer Mark* has unveiled deep problems in Jesus Studies, among them a trait I

[273.] Jeffery, *The Secret Gospel of Mark Unveiled*, 248.

call *reverse infallibility*—the evangelical who declares the Clement letter to be a transparent and execrable fraud today is likely to argue for the complete historicity of the resurrection or the reality of an imminent Rapture tomorrow.[274] True believers in the Judeo-Christian tradition are atavistically, almost genetically, predisposed to argue for the infallibility of texts—even a text roundly rejected as spurious still infallibly shows the bibliolater what he wants to see, tells him what he wants to hear, confirms his every suspicion and validates his every conclusion. To paraphrase Carlson, once you know what to look for, all you have to do is find it, and find "it" you most assuredly will, whether it is hidden signatures or dirty jokes, promoting an exegesis of solecistic misdirection that, to quote Jeffery, "sets up a circular argument from which there is no escape."

In retrospect it may come as a surprise that anyone within the New Testament studies establishment accepted Carlson's claim of forgery without waiting for confirmation or challenge on the part of qualified experts. Carlson set out to prove what he already believed—an odds-on recipe for academic debacle—and many within the academy were only too happy to accept his claims without question, falling into a swoon of credulity at the prospect that the pesky Smith had been discredited. That cherry-picking evidence to support a foregone conclusion is the very prescription for fraud seems never to have occurred to Carlson or his cheering squad.

[274.] The debased intellectual regime current among many evangelicals and its national consequences are subjects of frequent comment. Interested readers will find Mooney's *The Republican War on Science* covers the subject well.

The poison pill for New Testament studies generally and for *Longer Mark* specifically is theological commitment. That the New Testament is the gospel of Jesus Christ, humanity's Lord and Savior, is the bottom line for conservative Christians, and this conviction forms the sole *raison d'être* for New Testament study. Given this intellectual regime, the 'message of the Gospels' can never be falsified, scholarship as universally understood in other disciplines is reduced to a sham, and scholarly exchange among evangelicals and other literalists is no more about real scholarship than a drag show is about real women. Real scholarship in a real academic discipline includes *falsification of claims* as a concrete, ever-present possibility, a possibility that by definition does not exist within the mental framework of believer scholarship. The completely honest answer to Smith from conservative Christians would have been a simple retort on the order of "Jesus is my Lord, the Bible canon is divinely inspired, now butt out!" That answer, however intellectually vacuous, would have spared the lives of many trees. The position of a believer scholar in Jesus Studies is not dissimilar to that of a physician engaged in evaluating the efficacy of a new drug while collecting a tidy fee from the pharmaceutical company that produces it. The tendency to bias, whether conscious or not, is gravitational in its effect.

As Smith pointed out, the writings of Clement of Alexandria indicate that at least some Christian groups described their salvation in the language of the mystery religions and in support could produce evidence that Jesus himself as well as his apostles had clearly spoken in those terms. A period of revelation followed by initiation was one of several features that Alexandrian Christianity shared with mystery cults. Both the gnostic *Gospel of Judas* and the *Apocryphon of John*, for example, begin with the promise to reveal the "hidden words" of "secret teaching." Paul and his school peddled secrets and mysteries non-stop; Paul's gospel is the revelation of a mystery kept secret for ages;[275] he comes proclaiming the mystery of God,[276] the mystery hidden from ages [or *the Aeons*] and generations is now revealed to the saints.[277] The gospel is a mystery,[278] secret and hidden,[279] as is the faith,[280] the Christian religion,[281] the union of Christ and his church,[282] God's will,[283] Christ, another mystery,[284] the recalcitrance of the Jews, another,[285] and the explosion of competing Christian sects another yet.[286] From whence all this mystery if not from competition with the mystery cults of which Christianity was just another one of many? Secret and mystery were essential to the Christian sales pitch, the sizzle on the steak, the alluring new car smell cleverly applied to a high-mileage trade-in. Smell and sizzle aside, Christianity's

---

[275] Romans 16:25.
[276] 1 Corinthians 2:1.
[277] Colossians 1:26.
[278] Ephesians 6:19.
[279] 1 Corinthians 2:7.
[280] 1 Timothy 3:9.
[281] 1 Timothy 3:16.
[282] Ephesians 5:32.
[283] Ephesians 1:9.
[284] Colossians 4:3.
[285] Romans 11:25.
[286] 2 Thessalonians 2:7.

passion narratives shared the common denominator of the other mystery cults: *deliverance from death*.

It seems quite clear from the earliest Christian documents that some "advocated the moral irrelevance of the body,"[287] but the existing evidence does not permit us to confidently trace such an attitude back to ever elusive "historical Jesus," as Smith was well aware whatever his speculation on the matter. In a letter to Scholem, Smith had this to say about the reconstruction of the career of Jesus:

> As to Jesus, I should perhaps have emphasized more strongly that all accounts of his teaching and practice are conjectural, and I claim of my conjectures only that they fit the reports as well as any and better than most. Of course nothing can be proved about this subject. For practical purposes, the Gospels are our sole substantial evidence.[288]

Unfortunately for historians of early Christianity, the subjects of their study not only destroyed or neglected much more than they preserved, they searched out and burned the writings of their opponents, effectively erasing most of the history of primitive Christianity and contemporary reactions to it even as it progressed. "The burning of books was part of the advent and imposition of Christianity...By the middle of the fourth century, even Rome was virtually devoid of

---

[287.] See Jay Smith on 1 Corinthians 6:18 in the *Journal of Theological Studies* 59 (2008): 78-79.
[288.] Stroumsa, *Morton Smith and Gershom Scholem*, 160.

books."²⁸⁹ The scraps of evidence that can be sifted from the ashes of this cultural holocaust will never permit any more than a conjectural reconstruction of texts or events, and the teaching and initiation mentioned in *Longer Mark* must be considered within those severe limitations.

It is probable that all gospels began as local productions created for the needs of particular communities, reflecting their interpretations of Jesus. Some gospels, *Q* for instance—*a gospel that almost certainly existed but left no independent manuscript evidence*—were absorbed into other gospels and ceased to exist as independent books, a fate that might even have befallen Mark had circumstances been somewhat different. Other gospels, known only from their titles, succumbed to the vicissitudes of time and circumstance and vanished without a trace. It is possible that some were composed and never copied, or that only a very few copies, now lost, were ever made, a clear implication of the passing remark at John 21:25.

Nevertheless, Craig Evans, an evangelical New Testament scholar, finds it "unlikely that a different edition of Mark… could leave no traces in the manuscript tradition."²⁹⁰ To my knowledge, no copy of Marcion's edited gospel of Luke has survived, but no one seems to doubt that it existed. Origen knew of variant copies of Mark, mentioning *"the tax collector Leves"* (ο Λευης τελωνης) who followed Jesus but was not numbered among the apostles "except according to *certain of the copies* (τινα των αντιγραφων) of the gospel according to

---

²⁸⁹· Canfora, *The Vanished Library*, 192, 196.
²⁹⁰· Evans, *Ancient Gospel or Modern Forgery?*, 99.

Mark."[291] Luke, writing around the year 80, could already claim, "*many* attempted to produce an orderly narrative"[292] about the career of Jesus—where in the manuscript tradition is there any evidence of those *many* attempts? That early Christians were cranking out new gospels or new editions of existing gospels is not hard to suppose. Fragmentary remnants of gospels have appeared with some regularity, the Fayyum fragment, discovered in a collection in Vienna, in 1885, Oxyrhynchus 210, in 1899, Oxyrhynchus 840, 1908, Oxyrhynchus 1224, a Greek fragment of the *Gospel of Thomas*, in 1914, Papyrus Berlin 11710, 1923, Papyrus Egerton 2, 1935, Papyrus Merton 51, 1959, Oxyrhynchus 2949, discovered at the turn of the century, finally published in 1972, and the *Gospel of Judas* in 2006.

Against such a background, there is nothing remotely improbable about a special edition of Mark appearing for a generation or so among some Christians in Alexandria and disappearing, leaving only a partial quotation in the letter of Clement as the only surviving evidence of its brief existence. Brown notes of *Longer Mark*, "The only way the elders in [the Alexandrine] church could have restricted its hearing to theologically advanced Christians is by making very few copies and ensuring that those copies do not circulate."[293] If we know anything from textual criticism, it is that textual problems are better resolved by the discovery of more, hopefully better, text. However, the odds that a lost copy of

---

[291.] Origen, *Contra Celsum* I, 62.
[292.] Luke 1:1.
[293.] Brown, *Journal of Early Christian Studies* 16 (2008): 556.

Longer Mark still exists and awaits discovery seems infinitesimally small.

THE BELOVED DISCIPLE

Here is Mark 10:17-52 with the verses quoted by Clement restored to the text.

> After he set out on the road, a man came running up to him and *fell on his knees before him* (γονυπετησας αυτον) and asked him, "Good *Teacher* (διδασκαλε), what must I do to receive eternal life?" But Jesus said to him, "Why do you call me good? No one is good except God alone. You know the commandments: do not murder, do not commit adultery, do not steal, do not give false testimony, do not commit fraud, honor your father and your mother."
>
> He said to him, "Teacher, I have observed all these things since my childhood." *Gazing at him, Jesus loved him* (Ιησους εμβλεψας αυτω ηγαπησεν αυτον) and said to him, "You're missing one thing. Go sell everything you have and give it to the poor and you will have treasure in heaven. Come follow me." But he was appalled by Jesus' words and he went away offended, for he owned many possessions.
>
> Looking from person to person, Jesus said to his disciples, "How hard it will be for those who have wealth to enter the kingdom of God!"
>
> The disciples were astounded by his words, but Jesus said to them again, "Children, how hard it is to enter the kingdom of God! It is easier for a camel to go through the eye of a needle than for a rich man to

enter the kingdom of God!" They were overwhelmed with amazement and began to say to one another, "Who can be saved?" Looking at them intently, Jesus said, "Impossible for men, but not for God! For God, anything is possible."

Peter began to say to him, "Look, we have given up everything and followed you!"

Jesus answered, "Truly I say to you, there is no one who has left house or brothers or sisters or mother or father or children or fields on my account and on account of the good news who will not receive a hundred times as much now in this present time, houses and brothers and sisters and mothers and children and fields—with persecutions—and in the age to come eternal life. But many who are first will be last, and many last will be first."

They were on the road going up into Jerusalem and Jesus was going ahead of them. They were amazed and those who followed were afraid. He took the twelve aside again and began to tell them about the things that were soon to happen to him. "Look, we are going up to Jerusalem and the son of man will be handed over to the chief priests and the scribes and they will condemn him to death and they will hand him over to the Romans. They will ridicule him and spit on him and whip him and kill him, and after three days *he will raise himself* (αναστησεται)."

And they came to **Bethany** (Βηθανιαν) *and a certain woman whose brother had died came out and* **threw herself before** (προσεκυνησε) *Jesus and said to him, "Son of David, have mercy on me!" But the disciples rebuked her.* **Becoming** *angry* (οργισθεις),[294] *Jesus went off after her* **into the garden** (εις τον κηπον) *where the* **tomb** (μνημειον) *was and suddenly there was heard coming from the tomb* **a loud voice** (φωνη μεγαλη). *Approaching, Jesus* **rolled away the stone** (εκυλισε τον λιθον) *from the door of the tomb and immediately going into where* **the young man** (ο νεανισκος) *was, he stretched out his hand and raised him, holding his hand.*[295] **And gazing at him, the young man loved him** (ο νεανισκος εμβλεψας αυτω ηγαπησεν αυτον) *and began to plead with him that he might be with him.*

And going out of the tomb, they went into the young man's house, for he was rich. After six days, Jesus summoned him, and when evening came, the young man went to him **wearing a linen cloth** (περιβεβλημενος σινδονα) *over his naked body and he stayed with him that night for Jesus taught him the mystery of the kingdom of God. And then arising, he went to the far side of the Jordan.*

James and John, the sons of Zebedee, approached him and said to him, "Teacher, we want you to do whatever we ask you."

He said, "What do you want me to do for you?"

They said to him, "Let us sit, one at your right hand

[294.] As Meyer noted, οργιζω, *become angry*, is a near synonym of εμβριμαομαι, *become disturbed*, the verb used in the parallel story in John 11:33. (*Secret Gospels*, 139).

[295.] "...a story which reports the direct, physical method of taking the hand and literally raising the dead is probably more primitive than one which reports a raising by remote command... references to χειρ as an instrument of supernatural help are substantially more frequent in Mk. than in the later synoptics and Jn..." (Smith, *Clement of Alexandria*, 158).

and one at your left in your glory."

But Jesus said to them, "You don't know what it is you're asking for. Can you drink the cup I drink or be baptized with the baptism with which I will be baptized?"

They said to him, "We can."

So Jesus said to them, "The cup from which I drink, you will drink, and the baptism with which I am baptized, you will be baptized. But to sit at my right or at my left is not for me to give, but [is] for those for whom it has been prepared."

Now when the ten heard, they became incensed at James and John. Calling them all before him, Jesus said to them, "You know that those who appear to rule over the Gentiles lord it over them, and their great men exercise authority over them, but that is not how it is among you. Whoever wants to become great among you will be your servant, and whoever wants to be first among you will be a slave to everyone, because the son of man came not to be served, but to serve and give his life as a price paid for many."

They came to Jericho, *and the sister of the young man that Jesus loved and his mother and Salome were there, but Jesus did not agree to see them.* And as he was leaving Jericho with his disciples and a large crowd, *a blind beggar* (τυφλος προσαιτης), Bartimaeus, the son of Timaeus, was sitting by the road. When he heard that it was Jesus of Nazareth, he began to shout, saying, "Son of David, Jesus, take pity on me!" Many sternly warned him to shut up, but he shouted out even louder, "Son of David, take pity on me!"

So Jesus stopped and said, "Call him over." So they summoned the blind man, saying, "Take heart! Get up, he's calling you."

Throwing aside his coat, he got to his feet and went toward Jesus and Jesus said to him, "What do you want me to do for you?"

The blind man said, "Rabbouni, restore my sight!"

Jesus said to him, "Go. Your trust has healed you." And immediately his sight came back and he followed him down the road.

Here is John 11:1-44.

There was a certain sick man, Lazarus from *Bethany* (Βηθανιας), from the village of Mary and Martha his sister. This was the Mary who anointed the Lord with perfume and dried his feet with her hair. Her brother Lazarus fell sick. So the sisters sent for him, saying, "Listen, Lord, *the one you love* (ον φιλεις) is sick."

But when Jesus heard, he said to her, "This sickness will not result in death, but for the glory of God, so the Son of God may be glorified because of it." For Jesus loved Martha and her sister and Lazarus, but even though he heard he was sick he stayed in the place he was for two days. After that, he said to his disciples, "Let's go into Judea again."

The disciples began to say to him, "Rabbi, the Jews were just now seeking to stone you and you're going there again?"

Jesus answered, "Are there not twelve hours of daylight? Whoever walks in the daylight does not trip because he sees the light of this world. But whoever walks at night trips because the light is not in him." He said these things and after this he said to them, "Lazarus our friend has fallen asleep, but I am going there and I will wake him."

Therefore the disciples said to him, "Lord, if he has fallen asleep he will recover." Jesus had spoken about his death, but they thought he was speaking about the repose of sleep. Then Jesus spoke to them plainly, "Lazarus has died and for your sake I'm glad that we were not there so that you may believe. But let's go to him."

Thomas, who was called The Twin, said to his fellow disciples, "Let's go with him so we can die with him."

When Jesus arrived, he found him already four days in the tomb. Bethany was near Jerusalem, about two miles away. Many of the Jews had come out to Martha and Mary to console them about their brother.

When Martha heard that Jesus was on his way, she went to meet him, but Mary sat at home. Martha said to Jesus, "Lord, if you had been here, my brother would not have died, but even now I know that whatever you ask of God, God will grant you."

Jesus said to her, "Your brother will be raised."

Martha said to him, "I know he will be raised in the resurrection on the last day."

Jesus said to her, "*I am the resurrection* (Εγω ειμι η αναστασις) and the life. The one who believes in me will live even if he dies, and everyone who lives and believes in me will not die for all ages. Do you believe this?"

She said to him, "Yes, Lord, I have believed that you are the Christ, the Son of God, the One coming into the world." And after she said this, she went and called Mary her sister and told her privately, *"The Teacher (ο διδασκαλος)* is here and is calling you." And when she heard that, she got up quickly and went to him. Jesus had not come to the village yet, but was still in the place where Martha met him. The Jews who were with her in the house, and those comforting her, saw Mary get up suddenly and leave. They followed her, thinking that she was going to the tomb to cry there.

When Mary came to where Jesus was and saw him, *she fell at his feet (επεσεν αυτου προς τους ποδας)* and said to him, "Lord, if only you had been here, my brother would not have died."

When Jesus saw her crying and the Jews who came with her crying, *he was deeply moved by the spirit (ενεβριμησατο τω πνευματι)*[296] and *disturbed within*

---

[296] "The disappearance of the appeal to the son of David (a title Jn. never uses) entailed the disappearance of the rebuke and left the anger unexplained. John (or his source) therefore substituted the vague and pretentious και ενεβριμησατο κ.τ.λ., which seemed suitable as an introduction to the miracle because of the words' magical overtones…" (Smith, *Clement of Alexandria*, 154). Bonner's suggested translation, "the Spirit set him in a frenzy and he threw himself into disorder," emphasizes one of the "familiar features of the ordinary wonderworker's manner of

himself (εταραξεν εαυτον) and he said, "Where have you laid him?"

They said to him, "Lord, come and see." Jesus began to cry.

The Jews said, " See how he loved him!" But some of them said, "Couldn't he who opened *the blind man's eyes* (τους οφθαλμους του τυφλου) have done something so he might not have died?"

Then Jesus, again deeply moved within himself, came *to the tomb* (εις το μνημειον). It was a cave with *a stone* (λιθος) laying over it. Jesus said, "Take away the stone!"

Martha, the sister of the dead man, said to him, "Lord, by now he stinks, for it is four days!"

Jesus said to her, "Did I not tell you that if you believed you would see the glory of God?" So they removed the stone and Jesus raised his eyes and said, "Father I thank you because you heard me. I knew that you always hear me, but for the sake of the crowd standing here I said it so they may believe that you sent me." And after he said these things, he called out with *a loud voice* (φωνη μεγαλη),[297] "Lazarus! Out

---

operation." Of εμβριμαομαι, which means *snort* when applied to horses, Bonner noted, "when used of the behavior of a prophet, magician, or wonderworker, there is a strong presumption that they [εμβριμαομαι and ταρασσω, my note] imply frenzy or raving." (*Harvard Theological Review* 20 (1927): 171-181).

[297.] "The original significance of the cry from the tomb is probably indicated by the use of φωνη μεγαλη in Mk., where it occurs often at crises in the relations between spirits and men…the

here!" The dead man came out, his hands and feet wrapped with bindings and his face wrapped up *with a cloth* (σουδαριω). Jesus said to them, "Unbind him and let him go."

The restoration to canonical Mark of the verses quoted by Clement results in a more coherent story arc, but one which is still incomplete. At least with the missing verses back in place, we are now able to detect a *frame*, a parallel construction the editor of *Longer Mark* has used to identify a single character, the young man beloved by Jesus. The use of chiasmus to create epexegetical frames,[298] a peculiarity of Mark, is illustrated by this well-known example, better appreciated in Greek:

ειδεν σχιζομενους τους ουρανους και το πνευμα... (Mark 1:10)

εξεπνευσεν και το καταπετασμα του ναου εσχισθη... (Mark 15:37- 38)

he saw the heavens ripped apart and the spirit...

he expired and the curtain of the temple was ripped...

With the verses quoted by Clement restored to Mark, it is

φωνη μεγαλη is probably the cry of Death, departing from its prey." (Smith, *Clement of Alexandria*, 157). Compare similar imagery at Mark 1:26, 5:7, 15:34.

[298.] The interested reader is referred to John Dart's *Decoding Mark* for other possible examples.

immediately apparent that these are two versions of the same story—"the echoes of Secret Mark within canonical Mark help tell a coherent tale, and, what is more, tell one that is not merely parallel to but continuous with the story of Lazarus in John."[299] "These facts suggest that their material derives in part from an independent block of tradition which had some connection with an early stage in Jesus' career…This coincidence in order of so many events can hardly be accidental…their continual parallelism and substantial differences must be explained by supposition of a common source of which both authors used different developments… The source may have been in Aramaic and the differences may result in part from different translations."[300] Smith repeated this theory in a later article: "…an original Aramaic gospel had been twice translated into Greek; John used one translation, Mark another…"[301] thus accounting for both the similarities in vocabulary as well as the differences.

Both narratives are situated late in Jesus' career[302] when tensions with the Jewish authorities are about to result in his

---

[299] Fowler, *Journal of Higher Criticism* 5/1 (1998): 3-22.

[300] Smith, *Clement of Alexandria*, 161-162. "The close similarity between the stories…suggests that Mark and John have drawn upon a shared tradition…it is possible that this story is part of a more comprehensive source used independently by both evangelists." (Cameron, *The Other Gospels*, 68).

[301] Smith, *Harvard Theological Review* 75 (1982), 452.

[302] "Comparison of the Lazarus story in Jn. with that in the longer text of Mk. must begin with the observation…that both occur at the same place in Jesus' career." (Smith, *Clement of Alexandria*, 149).

arrest and execution,[303] and his disciples are understandably anxious.[304] Both stories take place in Bethany.[305] The healing of a blind man figures in both.[306] In both stories, Jesus is remembered as "the Teacher."[307] The man who meets Jesus on the road is evidently young and in good health—he ran up to Jesus—and Lazarus is evidently young and in good health, for the implication is that he will recover from his illness.[308] The young man of Mark is rich; Lazarus is also a man of means: he owns a house, is buried in a tomb, his funeral is well-attended, and his sister Mary anoints Jesus' feet with perfume worth 300 denarii, the equivalent of a year's wages for a common laborer.[309] Both the rich man of Mark and Lazarus are pious. Mark specifies that he is observant, and the fact that "many of the Jews" came down from Jerusalem to console Lazarus' sisters indicates that the family is well known and of good reputation in a devout community.[310] In Mark, Jesus says that anything is possible for God; in John's account Martha says that whatever Jesus wants, God will grant him.[311]

[303.] Mark 10:33, John 11:53, 57.

[304.] Mark 10:32, John 11:16.

[305.] Mark 11:1, John 11:1.

[306.] Mark 10:46-52, John 11:37.

[307.] Mark 10:17, John 11:28.

[308.] Mark 10:17, John 11:4. Matthew 19:20, 22, as already noted, specifies that the man on the road is a νεανίσκος (neaniskos), a *young man*. In John (20:4), the beloved disciple outruns Peter, arriving first at Jesus' tomb, a performance consistent with youth.

[309.] Mark 10:22, John 11:19, 31, 38, 12:3-5.

[310.] Mark 10:20, **John** 11:19.

[311.] Mark 10:27, John 11:22.

In a series of essays, Meyer noted a number of parallels between *Longer Mark* and John: the youth is from Bethany, his sister greets Jesus, a loud voice is mentioned, the stone sealing the tomb is removed, and Jesus then raises the youth.[312] That there might have been *two* youths, both raised at the same point in Jesus' career and sharing so many characteristics and circumstances, verges on the absurd. The conclusion is obvious: the rich young man of canonical Mark and *Longer Mark* and Lazarus of the gospel of John are one and the same.

Having allowed the text to confirm Lazarus' identity and the circumstances of his discipleship, we can now appreciate his role in the week preceding Jesus' arrest as described in John:

> The Passover of the Jews was near and many went up to Jerusalem from the surrounding country so they could purify themselves. They were looking for Jesus and were saying to one another as they stood in the temple, "What do you think? Will he dare come to the festival?" For the chief priests and the Pharisees had issued orders that anyone who knew where he was should reveal it so they could arrest him.
> Consequently, six days before Passover, Jesus came to Bethany where Lazarus was who Jesus had raised from the dead. They made a feast for him there. Martha served and Lazarus was one of those reclining with him. Mary took a litra of ointment, unadulterated spikenard—very valuable—and

---

[312.] Meyer, *Secret Gospels*, 139. The references are to John 11:1, 20, 39, 43-44.

anointed Jesus' feet with it and wiped his feet dry with her hair. The house was filled with the fragrance of the ointment.

A great multitude of the Jews found out he was there and came out, not only because of Jesus, but also that they might catch sight of Lazarus, who he had raised from the dead. So the chief priests planned on killing Lazarus as well. Because of him many of the Jews were breaking ranks and were beginning to believe in Jesus, for the crowd that had been with him when he called Lazarus from the tomb and raised him from the dead kept attesting to the event. That is why the crowd went out to meet him, because they heard he had performed the sign. Then the Pharisees said to one another, "You see! It's no use! Look, the whole world has gone off after him."[313]

From this account it is evident that Lazarus *redivivus* has become the main exhibit of Jesus' claim to miracle working, and by extension, the truth of Jesus' message. Lazarus' resurrection has become *the* occasion for belief—"so the Son of God may be glorified because of it."[314]

The identity of Lazarus as the rich young man, the disciple Jesus loved, also clears up a particularly enigmatic passage in the gospel of Mark—a passage Meyer described as "an interpretive nightmare"[315]—the mention of an event that happened during Jesus' arrest:

[313.] John 11:45-12:3, 9-11, 17-19.
[314.] John 11:4, 15, 26-27, 42.
[315.] Meyer, *Secret Gospels*, 117.

And they all fled, deserting him. *A certain young man* (νεανισκος τις) *went along* with him (συνακολουθει),³¹⁶ *wearing a linen cloth* (περιβεβλημενος σινδονα)³¹⁷ over his naked body, and *they seized* (κρατουσιν) him but he ran away naked, leaving them holding the linen cloth.³¹⁸

A number of parallels now appear between Jesus and the young man who flees naked at the time of Jesus' arrest, parallels noted with particular insight by Albert Van Hoye who points out that the same verb, κρατεω, *seize*, is used of the arrest of Jesus and the attempted arrest of the young man in the garden. The similar language is significant: Jesus and Lazarus are the two marked for death by the temple

---

316. The verb συνακολουθεω, to go along with, is used also in Mark 5:37: "he allowed no one but Peter to go along (συνακολουθησαι) with him." The verb signals an inner circle of disciples that Lazarus has joined; he is the beloved who, at Peter's behest, asks who will betray Jesus (John 13: 23-25), the one to whom Jesus entrusts his mother (John 19:26-27), and the first male to identify the risen Jesus in Galilee (John 21:7).

317. Linen features fairly often in magical ritual: "*Wrap* a naked boy *in linen* (σινδονιασις) from head to foot, clap [your hands], and ring a bell. Put the boy directly opposite the sun, and standing behind him, say the spell…" (*Papyri Graecae Magicae* IV, 89-91); "spread a clean *linen cloth* (σινδονιον) on the floor…and wrapping yourself up in the manner of a corpse, close your eyes…" (*Papyri Graecae Magicae* IV, 169-179). Raising the dead by magic is well attested.   Σινδων is an Egyptian loan word (Robertson, *A Grammar of the Greek New Testament in the Light of Historical Research*, 111). The reference in the magical papyri is likely to mummy cloth.

318. Mark 14:51-52.

authorities[319] and are the two seized by the temple police. Jesus is retained and Lazarus escapes.

The young man leaves a linen cloth in the hands of his would be captors; the same word, σινδων (sindōn), is used of his clothing both in Mark, in *Longer Mark*, and of Jesus' burial shroud—Joseph of Arimathea "*bought a linen shroud (αγορησας σινδονα), took [Jesus] down and wrapped him in the linen shroud (ενειλησεν τη σινδονι).*"[320] Van Hoye also noted the similarity between the young man (νεανισκος) in Gethsemane "*wearing a linen shroud*" (περιβεβλημενος σινδονα)[321] and the young man (νεανισκος) in Jesus' empty tomb "*wearing a white robe*" (περιβεβλημενον στολην λευκην).[322] Van Hoye concluded, "There is therefore reason to think that the numerous verbal correspondences which we have noted are not the result of pure chance, but manifest an intention."[323] Regarding the phrase περιβεβλημενος σινδονα επι γυμνου, *wearing a linen cloth over his naked* [body], Smith noted, "the occurrence of the phrase both in the longer and the canonical texts of Mk. can hardly be explained as an accident of free composition."[324]

[319.] John 11:53, 12:10.

[320.] Mark 15:46.

[321.] Mark 14:51.

[322.] Mark 16:5.

[323.] Van Hoye, "La fuite de jeune homme nu (Mc 14,51-52)," *Biblica* 52 (1971), 625-628. My translation of "Il y a donc lieu de penser que les nombreaux contacts verbaux que nous avons relevés ne sont pas un pur effet du hazard, mais manifestent une intention."

[324.] Smith, *Clement of Alexandria*, 116.

The numerous verbal correspondences seem to point to a specific individual who remains unnamed in Mark, but identified as Lazarus by John. The young man in Gethsemane is Lazarus, the beloved disciple, still dressed in his linen burial shroud. Both Miles Fowler and Michael Haran have suggested this identification.

> How would a crowd recognize which person standing among the numerous followers of Jesus is Lazarus? Mark 14:51 provides the answer that there could be no more impressive identification of Lazarus, nor any more vivid symbol of his resurrection, than his wearing a burial shroud.[325]

> The question must arise whether the manifestation of the glory was to be confined to Bethany or whether it was contemplated presenting Lazarus, dramatically and dressed so that he would instantly proclaim the miracle, in Jerusalem itself. Alternatively or concurrently, if, as the Gospels insist, Jesus was reconciled to or intent upon his own sacrifice, the prospect that Lazarus would be presented in Jerusalem as a sign of God's power might have been a central part of the mechanism by which the Jewish authorities were utterly drawn to act.[326]

Unfortunately for the temple authorities, word spread rapidly among the Passover crowds, a multitude that numbered well

---

[325.] Fowler, *Journal of Higher Criticism* 5/1 (1998): 20. Available online: http://www.depts.drew.edu/jhc/fowler.html.

[326.] Haren, *Biblica* 79 (1998): 525-531.

into the thousands, so that many who did not see the resurrection of Lazarus went thronging to Jesus, hoping to catch sight of Lazarus who, *dressed in his burial shroud*, publicly announced the reality of the miracle, and, if they were lucky, perhaps witness another miraculous sign.

John's account, composed much later than Mark, exhibits clear evidence of editing. John's version keeps mentioning "the Jews," a rather odd way of distinguishing characters since Jesus, his disciples, Mary, Martha, and Lazarus were all Jews—at this point, the Christians were becoming a separate sect in contradistinction to Judaism. John's account also betrays more advanced theologizing: Jesus is no longer the "son of man,"—likely derived from the Aramaic בר נשא, (bar nasha), "son of man," signifying nothing more than *a person*. (*Lazarus* also reflects a tendency of Galilean Aramaic to shorten and/or mispronounce words).[327] John's Jesus, on the other hand, has become "the Christ, the Son of God."

[327.] Vermes, *Journal of the Study of the New Testament* 1 (1978): 19-32. In the earliest tradition it is likely that Matthew 12:8 and parallels meant simply, "Man (בר נשא) is lord of the Sabbath."

Through death to life

The attraction of the mystery religions is easy enough to grasp. It is comforting to believe that the visible world is not the only world and that death is but a doorway to another life. We can see beyond this world and live beyond it as well. The Christian religion participates in this mythos: "What you sow does not come to life unless it dies."[328]

I have translated μετα τρεις ημερας αναστησεται as "after three days *he will raise himself*."[329] If construed as the middle voice—the middle voice in Greek indicates what the subject does *to or for himself*—αναστησεται means *he will raise himself*. However, all translators, accepting the claim that God raised Jesus from the dead, render the passage, *he will be raised*, reading the verb as passive in sense though middle in form. In defense of my translation, it must be pointed out that *Jesus clearly foretold that he would raise himself from the dead*:

> In response the Jews said to him, "What sign are you showing us that you are doing these things?"
> In reply Jesus said to them, "Destroy this temple and in three days I will raise it."[330]
> Then the Jews said, "This temple was built in forty-six years and in three days you will raise it?" But he said that about the temple of his body.[331]

---

[328] 1 Corinthians 15:376.

[329] Mark 10:34.

[330] και εν τρισιν ημεραις εγερω αυτον: "and in three days I will raise it."

[331] John 2:18-21.

"Instead of displaying another sign on the spot, Jesus promises one—it will be his greatest and will give the best apology imaginable for his death. That he is to accomplish his own resurrection is virtually unique in the N[ew]T[estament]. If there was any doubt that he had been alluding to his own death (and resurrection), it is dispelled by the formula, *in three days*."[332]

The gospel of John is quite explicit on this point:

> This is why the Father loves me, because I lay aside my life in order that I might take it up again. No one takes it from me, but I lay it aside of my own volition. I have the authority to lay it down and I have authority to take it up again. This is the order I received from my Father.[333]

It is crucial to note the claim of *authority*: εξουσιαν εχω θειναι αυτην και εξουσιαν εχω παλιν λαβειν αυτην, "I have the authority to lay it down, and I have the authority to take it up again." After this surprising announcement the Jews respond: δαιμονιον εχει και μαινεται, "He has a demon and he's raving!"—a charge that Jesus is a magician. The contrast is clear: Jesus claims to have *authority*, his opponents claim he has a *demon*. Both are claims that Jesus can perform amazing works of power, the question, as the context reveals,[334] concerns the source of Jesus' power.

[332.] Miller, *The Complete Gospels*, 187 (footnote on John 2:19).
[333.] John 10:17-18.
[334.] John 10:19-21.

Significantly, the gospel of Mark contains very similar wording regarding the death and resurrection of the Son of Man: μετα τρεις ημερας αναστησεται, "after three days he will raise himself."[335] After the first such prediction Mark notes that the disciples did not understand what Jesus' was talking about and were afraid to ask.[336] But if Jesus 'merely' predicted that a divine agency would raise the Son of Man from the dead as the Old Testament prophets had raised people from the dead and as Jesus himself raised people from the dead, what was there to misunderstand? To the best of my knowledge there is no text within normative Judaism that speaks of a person raising *himself* from the dead.

The remarkable notion that Jesus could raise himself from the dead is mentioned in a letter of Ignatius, an early martyr, composed around the beginning of the 2nd century. Writing against the Docetist heresy, which claimed that Jesus was a spirit that only appeared to suffer in the flesh, Ignatius says, "He suffered all these things on our account that we might be saved, and he truly suffered *as also he truly raised himself*"—ως και αληθως ανεστησεν εαυτου.[337] In this case, there is no debate about how the verb might be construed; the reflexive form is the clearest possible way of stating that Jesus raised himself. That raising oneself from the dead is exactly the sort of thing a magician might do is confirmed by Hippolytus' accusation that Simon Magnus made precisely such a claim.[338]

---

[335] Mark 9:31.
[336] Mark 9:32.
[337] Ignatius, *Ad Smyrnaeos*, II.
[338] Tuzlak, *Magic and Ritual in the Ancient World*, 419.

Christianity's opponents knew of this remarkable prediction. Origen felt obligated to repeat it in his defense against Celsus, but ascribed it to "false witnesses" who testified at Jesus' trial:

> At last, two came forward and stated, "This man said, 'I can tear down the temple of God and in three days build it up.'"[339]

Nevertheless, Origen clearly believed that Jesus *"quickly departed from the body* (ταχα...εξεληλυθεν απο του σωματος) that he might keep it intact and that his legs might not be broken like those of the robbers crucified with him" while revealing in the same context that Celsus "equated [Jesus'] wonders with sorceries" (κοινοποιειν αυτα προς τας γοητειας).[340] That Celsus believed the resurrection to be an act of magic is clear: "[Jesus] foretold that after dying *he will raise himself* (αναστησεται)," and offers the claim as a case of "exploiting others *by deceit* (πλανη)." Accordingly, Jesus appears post mortem to "a woman in a frenzy" (γυνη παροιστρος) "and some others under the same spell" (και ει τις αλλος των εκ της αυτης γοητειας).[341]

The gospel of Mark as we now have it contains three predictions of Jesus' death and if read from a strictly grammatical point of view it appears that Jesus' prediction of

---

[339.] δυναμαι καταλυσαι τον ναον του θεου και δια τριων ημερων οικοδομησαι: "I can tear down the temple of God and in three days build it up." *Contra Celsum, Præfatio* I.

[340.] Origen, *Contra Celsum* II, 16.

[341.] Ibid, II, 54-55.   Γυνη παροιστρος could be translated "a woman in estrus" (from οιστραω, *to be in a frenzy* or "in heat").

self-resurrection becomes progressively more stark in each. In the first instance, Jesus' prediction is characterized as *teaching* —και ηρξατο διδασκειν αυτους, "he began to teach them" (for the first time?)—that the Son of Man would be killed "and after three days *rise* (αναστηναι)."[342] The second prediction is also a *teaching*—"he taught (εδιδασκεν) his disciples"—the Son of Man would be killed and "after three days *raise himself* (αναστησεται)."[343] In the third occurrence, Jesus separates the twelve from his entourage—"calling the twelve aside again"— and lays out in greater detail what he will endure. He will be mocked, spit on, flogged and killed, "*and after three days he will raise himself* (και μετα τρεις ημερας αναστησεται)."[344] Jesus' *teaching* is preparing his disciples both for death and victory over death. It seems plausible that the "mystery of the kingdom of God"[345] imparted to Lazarus involved the necessity of Jesus' own death and resurrection which the resurrection of Lazarus prefigured.

The point of the Lazarus story is plain: "I *am* the resurrection and the life."[346] Jesus has the keys to Death and the Grave,[347] hence his authoritative command when Lazarus, bound hand and foot, emerges from the tomb: "*Release him* (λυσατε αυτον) and let him go!"[348] The Lazarus narrative emphasizes Jesus'

---

[342] Mark 8:31.
[343] Mark 9:31.
[344] Mark 10:32-34.
[345] See the text of the letter to Theodore, page 21.
[346] John 11: 25.
[347] Revelation 1:18.
[348] John 11:44.

power through a number of details: Jesus delays his arrival, allowing Lazarus to die and be buried. By the time he finally arrives, the corpse has begun to stink. The writer wants us to know that Lazarus is dead. *Really* dead. Like Jesus himself, Lazarus is raised, not from his death bed[349] or from a bier,[350] *but from a tomb after a span of days.* Given this setting, the significance of the linen sheet is clear: "In Mystical Mark, the three young men are clearly the same individual. And his linen sheet does make sense as a burial shroud. He wears it in the evening after six days to signify what Jesus is teaching him—that the way to life (the white robe) is through self-abandonment and death (the burial shroud)."[351]

According to the gospel of John, Peter and the beloved disciple are the first men to witness the empty tomb, but the beloved disciple, who by now has proven to be fleet of foot, beats Peter to the tomb, becoming the first male witness of the resurrection. It is no coincidence that the women who first arrive at Jesus' tomb find there "a young man clothed in a white robe" who announces, "He has been raised. He is not here."[352]

It seems likely that an inner circle saw the raising of Lazarus as an enacted parable of Jesus' self-resurrection. That Mark and John preserve so many parallels between the raising of Lazarus and the resurrection of Jesus suggests that some

---

[349] Mark 5:39-42.
[350] Luke 7:11-16.
[351] Brown, *The Fourth R* 25/6, 9.
[352] Compare Mark 16:6 and John 20:4.

early disciples were eager to find (or invent) such correspondences—"Interpretation of the Lazarus story as foreshadowing Jesus' resurrection may have led to the location of Lazarus' tomb, too, in a κηπος [garden]."[353] The eventual death of Lazarus is the motivation for the composition of the second ending of John; was Lazarus' death thought by some to put the post mortem life of Jesus himself in question?

> Turning around, Peter saw the disciple Jesus loved following them, the one who leaned against Jesus' chest during the supper and said, "Lord, who is the one betraying you?" When Peter saw him, he said to Jesus, "Lord, what about him?"
> Jesus said to him, "If I wish him to remain until I come, what do you care? You follow me." Therefore the word went out among the brothers that the disciple would not die. But Jesus did not say of him, "He will not die," but "If I wish for him to remain until I come, what do you care?"[354]

It is possible that it was Peter himself who put the word out that the beloved disciple would not die. When the beloved disciple identified the stranger on the shore as the risen Jesus, Peter "heard that it was the Lord," threw on some clothes, jumped into the sea, and swam to shore rather than wait.[355] "John 21:23a suggests that there is speculation within the

---

[353] Smith, *Clement of Alexandria*, 105.
[354] John 21:20-23.
[355] John 21:7-8.

earliest Jesus movement—especially by Peter—regarding the mortality of this disciple, whoever he is…if, perhaps even in historical fact, Peter went around saying that a certain youth would never die, and that youth did die, such an embarrassment might explain why the synoptic gospels omit stories about Jesus raising his friend from the dead."[356] Fowler's conclusion is supported by the text of Mark which everywhere assumes the imminence of the Parousia: "Truly I tell you that there are some standing here who will by no means taste death before they see *the kingdom of God has arrived in power* (την βασιλειαν του θεου εληλυθυιαν εν δυναμει)."[357]

Clement may have been accurate when he said that Mark wrote down "the things the Lord did while Peter was in Rome." *Longer Mark* may have contained a complete recounting of the story of Jesus and Lazarus that was subsequently suppressed to protect the sensibilities of the church. Later writers, unfamiliar with the story or uncomfortable with its details, ignored it. It has no doubt

---

[356] Fowler, *Journal of Higher Criticism* 5.1 (1998), 9.

[357] Repeated by Matthew (16:28) and Luke (9:27). It is clear from Paul's letter to the Thessalonians that the first generation of Christians believed at least some would survive until the Second Coming (3:13, 4:15, 17-18, 5:23). "…in the first generations Christianity was a millenarian movement…The earliest Christian communities stood in the mainstream of Jewish apocalyptic thinking…The kingdom would happen in the near future; it would happen as an event in history, indeed as the final event of history in its present mode." (Gager, *Kingdom and Community*, 32, 43).

struck many as strange that the story of Lazarus, the most emotionally resonant of the gospel stories, appears only in John and even there it is incompletely told.

LEFT BEHIND

In the early 1920's, in one of those proud moments for which the American South is justifiably famous, one John Washington Butler, a tobacco farmer who knew nothing about evolution, wrote a law that made the teaching of evolution illegal in Tennessee. The law was soon challenged in court in the famous "Scopes Monkey Trial" of 1925, during which the Bible quoting prosecution, frequently depicted in newspaper cartoons, became the object of international ridicule.

Following the Scopes debacle, Christian fundamentalists retreated and began to plan a cultural counteroffensive. "By 1930, there were at least fifty fundamentalist Bible colleges in the United States. During the Depression years, another twenty-six were founded…Fundamentalists also formed their own publishing and broadcasting empires."[358] Nearly a century later, fundamentalism in America has experienced resurgence. Liberty "University," was founded in 1971 by Baptist preacher Jerry Falwell, who in the 1960's ran the radio program "The Old-Time Gospel Hour," a program that regularly featured interviews with segregationists. Today the school boasts a Center for Creation Studies[359]—it seems to me that for the sake of consistency Falwell U would also boast a Center for Resurrection Studies. At Biola University, a major fundamentalist school, a bachelor's in biological science

---

[358.] Armstrong, *The Battle for God*, 214.
[359.] http://www.liberty.edu/academics/arts-sciences/creation/

calls for no less than 30 credit hours in "Bible," including two courses in theology.[360]

The Division of Natural Science at Bob Jones "University," a school that until recently forbid interracial dating, produces widely-used textbooks that teach "young Earth" creationism. The Institute for Creation Research, part of the School of Biblical Apologetics in Dallas, Texas, is home to a Christian celebrity, John D. Morris, Ph.D., who has predictably connected the horror of homosexuality to the evil of evolution and sees the progress of legal parity for gay Americans "as part of a larger, even more insidious plot."[361] Dr. Morris also poses the question, "Are Plants Alive?"—a question that I'll bet you thought had been answered—and reveals the conclusion, based on his Bible study, that, "while *biologically* alive, plants are therefore not *Biblically* 'living.'"[362] First grade biology aside, what's really crucial is not what your lying eyes may be telling you, but what Dr. Morris thinks Genesis says. Evangelicals, whose religious fairyland is constantly threatened with inundation by a sea of facts, have retreated to castles of illusion, schools where you flunk out of if you get the answers right.

Several years ago a coworker—a college-educated, professionally licensed coworker—mentioned that he planned to take his family to Los Angeles for several days. I asked if he'd ever visited the Page Museum, site of the La Brea tar

---

[360.] http://www.biola.edu/registrar/degree_requirements/undergrad/2014-2015/BSGB.pdf.
[361.] http://www.icr.org/article/1081/.
[362.] http://www.icr.org/article/1099.

pits, with its amazing collection of fossils. I happened to mention that some theorize the early culture that created Clovis points over 10,000 years ago might have contributed to the extinction of North American megafauna. My coworker promptly informed me, in all seriousness, that such a theory simply wasn't possible because the Earth is only 6000 years old and that the mammoths and mastodons had probably disappeared "because the dinosaurs ate them." I thought of mentioning that, oddly enough, no dinosaur bones have been recovered from La Brea, but given the manic glitter in his eye I opted to drop the subject.

It is, I believe, no coincidence that opposition to Smith's discovery has mainly come from staunchly evangelical and Catholic quarters. Historically speaking, it could have been no other way. If there is one thing that Bible colleges have taught to perfection, it is contempt for normal canons of evidence. Among evangelicals, belief in the improbable is a mark of faith, the more improbable, the more pure the faith. Long before Smith published, true believers were convinced they faced a massive, international conspiracy bent on their defeat, a conspiracy of atheists, Jews, communists, homosexuals, humanists, Hollywood liberals, higher critics, scientists, secular institutions and, of course, the media. Primed to interpret reality in terms of conspiracy and to see themselves as its perpetual martyrs, it is only natural that so many have framed the arguments against authenticity in the language of duplicity, subterfuge and intrigue. Homosexuality generally being a major source of evangelical and Catholic hand-wringing and existential angst, it is little surprise that Smith's detractors have focused like a laser on his sexual orientation.

The entrenched conservative Christian advocates of the forgery hypothesis are clearly stuck on replay, recycling previously failed or dubious arguments in a self-replicating meme—I regard Evans,[363] and Watson[364] among others as particularly representative of this dead-ended approach. For a critique of the evangelical tendency to disparage non-canonical texts generally, see Burke.[365]

Craig A. Evans, a professor at Acadia Divinity College, a Baptist seminary in Nova Scotia, is walking, talking example of the artless mendacity typical of evangelical casuistry. In 2006, Evans penned *Fabricating Jesus*, an examination of extra-canonical gospels. In his brief discussion of "Secret" Mark, Evans starts off by fabricating evidence, claiming that "in [the first Marcan fragment] Jesus raises a dead man, and then later, in the nude, instructs the young man in the mysteries of the

---

[363] Evans, "Morton Smith and the Secret Gospel of Mark: Exploring the Grounds for Doubt," *Ancient Gospel or Modern Forgery?*, 75-100. For the rebuttal, Brown & Pantuck, "Craig Evans and Secret Gospel of Mark: Exploring the Grounds for Doubt," *Ancient Gospel or Modern Forgery?*, 101-134 as well as

[364] Watson, "Beyond Suspicion: On the Authorship of the Mar Saba Letter and the Secret Gospel of Mark," *Journal of Theological Studies* 61 (2010): 128-170. For the rebuttal, Paananen, http://salainenevankelista.blogspot.com/ 2010/07/close-look-at-francis-watsons-beyond.html

[365] Burke, "Heresy Hunting in the New Millennium," *Studies in Religion/Sciences Religieuses* 39 (2010): 405-420. A condensed version is available at www.sbl-site.org/publications/article.aspx?Articled=787.

kingdom of God."³⁶⁶ What the text in question *actually* says is, "After six days, Jesus summoned him and when evening came, the young man went to him wearing a linen cloth over his naked body and he stayed with him that night, for Jesus taught him the mystery of the kingdom of God." There is no mention of Jesus teaching "in the nude," nor, for that matter of the young man being nude. "Wearing a linen cloth" does not constitute nudity any more than wearing gym shorts or swim trunks. A nude baptismal ritual, *inferred by Smith*, is not, in fact, mentioned in *Longer Mark*, but after being washed, a nude corpse being prepared for burial might very well been wrapped in a linen shroud and nothing else, hence the symbolism.

Another lie follows hard on the heels of the first: "no one besides Smith has actually studied the physical document." In fact, Smith did not use the "physical document" for his studies. He used his photos. Evans is also clearly confused about the nature of the photographic evidence itself, claiming that "color photographs of the document have given experts in the science of the detection of forgeries the opportunity to analyze the handwriting of the document and compare it with samples of the handwriting of the late Professor Smith."³⁶⁷ In point of fact, there were no "experts in the science of the detection of forgeries" involved. Stephen Carlson *has no training in document verification* or in paleography, and Julie Edison, whom he 'consulted,' could not even recite the Greek alphabet. Nor did Carlson reference the color photos; he

---

³⁶⁶· Evans, *Fabricating Jesus*, 95.
³⁶⁷· Ibid, 95.

worked from the inadequate halftones reproduced in Smith's *Clement of Alexandria*. At this point I would offer the distinguished professor Evans a challenge that even a Baptist Sunday school teacher might perform: turn to pages 448 through 453 of Smith's scholarly work and with a magnifying lens confirm for yourself that *the writing and the background on which it appears consist of dots that merely approximate the writing of the letter to Theodore. These reproductions are not photographs.* As a further point of fact, it was precisely *by examining the color photographs* of the letter to Theodore that Viklund utterly demolished Carlson's amateur effort.

Evans persists in characterizing Edison as "a professional handwriting expert,"[368] who could presumably make some material contribution to the debate on authenticity, despite her statement, "…my knowledge of early Christianity is basic at best. And I have limited knowledge of the Greek alphabet."[369] Whatever Edison's qualifications in document examination, Evans is unable to comprehend the simple fact that Edison *never examined a document*. What Edison 'examined' were *halftone reproductions of a document in a language she couldn't read*. Perhaps it bears reiterating to Dr. Evans that a woman's no means no, and that he should stop imploring.

At least it appears that Evans is currently creating a little wiggle room between himself and the incredible shrinking document expert. His current story is that Carlson "does not

---

[368.] Evans, *Ancient Gospel or Modern Forgery?*, 91.

[369.] Brown & Pantuck, *Ancient Gospel or Modern Forgery?*, 123. Scott Brown and Allan Pantuck have published a thorough refuta-tion of Evans' claims in the above-referenced volume (101-134).

regard himself as a handwriting expert per se," but states that Carlson's "expertise"—*for which there is no evidence*—"should not be quickly dismissed."[370] The sad fact is not that Carlson's illusory "expertise" is being dismissed, but that it was ever imagined in the first place.

The hope that the Clement letter might be discredited by forensic demonstrations appears to be fading, but another tactic has recently been resuscitated, the attempt to link Smith's discovery to the plot of Christian thrillers published before Smith visited Mar Saba, particularly Hunter's book, *The Mystery of Mar Saba*, published in 1940. Hunter's novel, a fervid evangelical melodrama, relates the discovery of fake text planted in the monastery by evil Nazis to discredit Christianity, a plot that supposedly "foreshadowed"[371] Smith's own discovery, very likely through the same mechanism that random passages from the Hebrew Bible supposedly foreshadowed the career of Jesus. It has obviously not occurred to Smith's detractors to wonder why a person of his temperament would have bothered to read hundreds of pages of fictional dreck or how the supposedly diabolical Smith could be so simpleminded that he would merely duplicate the plot of a popular novel. This allegation, which is even more tedious than the novel on which it's based, has been addressed here[372] and here.[373]

---

[370] Evans, *Ancient Gospel or Modern Forgery?*, 92.
[371] Evans, *Fabricating Jesus*, 97.
[372] Pantuck, www.bib-arch.org/scholars-study/secret-mark-handwriting-response-pantuck.pdf.
[373] Smith, *The Temple Sleep of the Rich Young Ruler*, 262-265.

The academic future of *Longer Mark* appears bleak. I would hazard a guess that whatever the actual enrollment numbers, New Testament studies has fallen on lean times and I would assume that Jesus Studies among evangelicals, already rife with special pleading, question begging and pseudo-academic nonsense, attracts and retains fewer and fewer great minds. Some of the debaters in the "Secret" Mark controversy were apparently boys who loved Sunday school a bit more than usual and have just refused to give it up. I suspect the flaxen-haired Jesus who walked on the waves was for them what Tyrannosaurus rex was for other boys.

Short of some serendipitous manuscript discovery that breaks the current impasse, it seems unlikely that the teapot tempest swirling around *Longer Mark* will ever see a definitive resolution. The debate is, after all, a forty-year-old *religious* ruckus in which scholarship has played a badly tuned second fiddle.

REFERENCES

Achtemeier, Paul J. "Review of Smith," *Journal of Biblical Literature* 93 (1974): 625-628.
Armstrong, Karen. *The Battle for God*, 2000, Alfred A. Knopf.
Barton, Stephen C. *Discipleship and Family Ties in Mark and Matthew*, 1994, Cambridge University Press.
Bauckham, Richard. "Salome the Sister of Jesus, Salome the Disciple of Jesus, and the Secret Gospel of Mark," *Novum Testamentum* 33 (1991): 245-275.
Betz, Hans Dieter (ed). *The Greek Magical Papyri in Translation Including the Demotic Spells*, 1986, University of Chicago Press.
Bonner, Campbell. "Traces of Thaumaturgical Techniques in the Miracles," *Harvard Theological Review* 20/3 (1927): 171-181.
Brown, Scott G. *Mark's Other Gospel: Rethinking Morton Smith's Controversial Discovery*, 2005, Wilfrid Laurier University Press.
—. "The Question of Motive in the Case Against Morton Smith," *Journal of Biblical Literature* 125/2 (2006): 351-383.
—. "Factualizing the Folklore: Stephen Carlson's Case Against Morton Smith," *Harvard Theological Review* 99 (2006): 291-327.
—. "Reply to Stephen Carlson," *Expository Times* 117 (2006): 144-149.
—. "The Secret Gospel of Mark Unveiled: An Essay Review," *Review of Biblical Literature* (9/15/2007): http//www.bookreviews.prg/pdf/5627_5944.pdf.
—. "The Letter to Theodore: Stephen Carlson's Case Against Clement's Authorship," *Journal of Early Christian Studies* 16/4 (2008): 535-572.
—. "The Mystical Gospel of Mark: Part One," *The Fourth R* 25/6 (November-December, 2012), 5-10.
—. "The Mystical Gospel of Mark: Part Two," *The Fourth R*, 26/1 (January-February, 2013), 5-24.

—. "Behind the Seven Veils, I: The Gnostic Life Setting of the Mystic Gospel of Mark," *Ancient Gospel or Modern Forgery? The Secret Gospel of Mark in Debate*, T. Burke (ed), 2013, Cascade Books.
Brown, Scott G. & Allan J. Pantuck. "Stephen Carlson's Questionable Questioned Document Examination," *Salainen evankelista* (April 14, 2010). http://salainenevankelista.blogspot.com/2010/04/stephen-carlsons-questionable.html.
—. "Craig Evans and the Secret Gospel of Mark: Exploring the Grounds for Doubt," *Ancient Gospel or Modern Forgery? The Secret Gospel of Mark in Debate*, T. Burke (ed), 2013, Cascade Books.
Bruce, Frederick F. "The 'Secret' Gospel of Mark," The Ethel M. Wood Lecture (11/02/1974), Athlone Press.
Burke, Tony. "Heresy Hunting in the New Millennium," *Studies in Religion/Sciences Religiuses* 39 (2010): 405-420.
—. "Introduction," *Ancient Gospel or Modern Forgery? The Secret Gospel of Mark in Debate*, T. Burke (ed), 2013, Cascade Books.
Buttersworth, G.W. *Clement of Alexandria: The Exhortation to the Greeks*, 1919, Harvard University Press.
Cameron, Ron (ed). *The Other Gospels: Non-Canonical Gospel Texts*, 1982, The Westminster Press.
Canfora, Luciano. *The Vanished Library: A Wonder of the Ancient World*, M. Ryle (tr), 1987, University of California Press.
Carlson, Stephen C. "Clement of Alexandria on the 'Order' of the Gospels," *New Testament Studies* 47/1 (2001): 118-125.
—. *The Gospel Hoax: Morton Smith's Invention of Secret Mark*, 2005, Baylor University Press.
—. "Reply to Scott Brown," *Expository Times* 117 (2006): 185-188.
Chadwick, Henry. *Origen: Contra Celsum*, 1965, Cambridge University Press.
Collins, Derek. *Magic in the Ancient Greek World*, 2008, Wiley.
Conner, Robert P. *Jesus the Sorcerer: Exorcist and Prophet of the Apocalypse*, 2006, Mandrake of Oxford.

—. *Magic in Christianity: From Jesus to the Gnostics*, 2014, Mandrake of Oxford.
Conybeare, F.C. Philostratus: *The Life of Apollonius of Tyana*, II, 1912, Harvard University Press.
Cosaert, Carl P. *The Text of the Gospels in Clement of Alexandria*, 2008, Society of Biblical Literature.
Criddle, A.H. "On the Mar Saba Letter Attributed to Clement of Alexandria," *Journal of Early Christian Studies* 3/2 (1995): 215-220.
Crossan, John D. *Four Other Gospels: Shadows on the Contour of Canon*, 1985, Polebridge Press.
—. *The Historical Jesus: The Life of a Mediterranean Jewish Peasant*, 1991, HarperCollins.
Daniel, Robert W. & Franco Maltomini (eds). *Supplementum Magicum* I (1990) & II (1992), Westdeutscher Verlag.
Dart, John. *Decoding Mark*, 2003, Bloomsbury Academic Press.
Deutsch, Celia. "Visions, Mysteries, and the Interpretive Task: Text Work and Religious Experience in Philo and Clement," *Experientia: Inquiry into Religious Experience in Early Judaism and Early Christianity*, Vol. I, Flanery, F., et al. (eds), 2008, Society of Biblical Literature.
Ehrman, Bart. *Lost Christianities: The Battle for Scripture and the Faiths We Never Knew*, 2003, Oxford University Press.
—. "Response to Charles Hedrick's Stalement," *Journal of Early Christian Studies* 11/2 (2003): 155-163.
—. *Forged: Writing in the Name of God—Why the Bible's Authors Are Not Who We Think They Are*, 2011, HarperOne.
Eitrem, Samson. *Some Notes on the Demonology in the New Testament*, 2nd ed., 1966, Symbolae Osloenses, 12.
Ellens, J. Harold. *Review of Biblical Literature* (6/01/2009): http://www.bookreviews.org/pdf/5627_7785.pdf.
Evans, Craig A. *Fabricating Jesus: How Modern Scholars Distort the Gospels*, 2006, InterVarsity Press.
—. "Morton Smith and the Secret Gospel of Mark: Exploring the Grounds for Doubt," *Ancient Gospel or Modern Forgery?*, 75-100.

Eyer, Shawn. "The Strange Case of the Secret Gospel According to Mark: How Morton Smith's Discovery of a Lost Letter by Clement of Alexandria Scandalized Biblical Scholarship," *Alexandria: The Journal for the Western Cosmological Tradition* 3 (1995): 103-129.

Farnell, Lewis R. *The Cults of the Greek States*, II, 1896, Clarendon Press.

Flint, Valerie. "The Demonization of Magic and Sorcery in Late Antiquity: Christian Redefinition of Pagan Religions," *Witchcraft and Magic in Europe: Ancient Greece and Rome*, B. Ankarloo & S. Clark (eds), 1999, University of Pennsylvania Press.

Foster, Paul. "Secret Mark," *The Non-Canonical Gospels*, P. Foster (ed), 2008, T&T Clark.

Fowler, Miles. "Identification of the Bethany Youth in the Secret Gospel of Mark with Other Figures Found in Mark and John," *The Journal of Higher Criticism* 5/1 (1998): 3-22.

Furguson, Everett. *Baptism in the Early Church: History, Theology, and Liturgy in the First Five Centuries*, 2009, Wm. B. Eerdmans.

Gager, John G. *Kingdom and Community: The Social World of Early Christianity*, 1975, Prentice-Hall.

Grafton, Anthony. "Gospel Secrets: The Biblical Controversies of Morton Smith," *The Nation*, 1/26/2009.

Haren, Michael J. "The Naked Young Man: A Historian's Hypothesis on Mark 14, 51-52," *Biblica* 79 (1998): 525-531.

Harris, William V. "A Bible fantasy," *Times Literary Supplement* 5455, 10/19/2007, 23.

Hedrick, Charles W. "The Secret Gospel of Mark: Stalemate in the Academy," *Journal of Early Christian Studies* 11/2 (2003): 133-145.

—. "An Amazing Discovery," *Biblical Archaeology Review*, November/December (2009): 44-48.

—. "Secret Mark: Moving on from Stalemate," *Ancient Gospel or Modern Forgery? The Secret Gospel of Mark in Debate*, T. Burke (ed), 2013, Cascade Books.

Hull, John M. *Hellenistic Magic and the Synoptic Tradition*, 1974, SCM Press.

Humphrey, Hugh M. *From Q to "Secret" Mark: A Composition History of the Earliest Narrative Theology*, 2006, T&T Clark.

Jay, Jeff. "A New Look at the Epistolary Framework of the Secret Gospel of Mark," *Journal of Early Christian Studies* 16/4 (2008): 573-597.

Jeffery, Peter. *The Secret Gospel of Mark Unveiled: Imagined Rituals of Sex, Death, and Madness in a Biblical Forgery*, 2007, Yale University Press.

—. "Clement's Mysteries and Morton Smith's Magic," *Ancient Gospel or Modern Forgery? The Secret Gospel of Mark in Debate*, T. Burke (ed), 2013, Cascade Books.

Johnston, Sarah I. *Restless Dead: Encounters Between the Living and the Dead in Ancient Greece*, 1999, University of California Press.

Klijn, A.E.J. "Jewish Christianity in Egypt," *The Roots of Egyptian Christianity*, B.A. Pearson & J.E. Goehring (eds), 1986, Fortress Press.

Koester, Helmut. *Ancient Christian Gospels: Their History and Development*, 1992, T&T Clark.

—. "Was Morton Smith a Great Thespian and I a Complete Fool?" *Biblical Archaeology Review* 35/6 (2009): 54-58, 88-90.

Kraeling, Carl H. "Was Jesus Accused of Necromancy?" *Journal of Biblical Literature* 59 (1940): 147-157.

MacMullen, Ramsey. *Christianizing the Roman Empire: AD 100-400*, Yale University Press.

Martin, Dale. *Sex and the Single Savior: Gender and Sexuality in Biblical Interpretation*, 2005, Editions Errance.

Meyer, Marvin. *Secret Gospels: Essays on Thomas and the Secret Gospel of Mark*, 2003, Trinity Press International.

—. "The Young Streaker in Secret and Canonical Mark," *Ancient Gospel or Modern Forgery? The Secret Gospel of Mark in Debate*, T. Burke (ed), 2013, Cascade Books.

Meyer, Marvin & Richard Smith. *Ancient Christian Magic: Coptic Texts of Ritual Power*, 1994, Harper San Francisco.
Mixner, David. "LGBT History: The Decade of Lobotomies, Castration and Institutions," http://www.davidmixner.com/2010/07/lgbt-history-the-decade-of-lobotomies-castration-and-institutions.html.
Mullins, Terence Y. "Papias and Clement on Mark's Two Gospels," *Vigiliae Christianae* 30/3 (1976): 189-192.
Osborne, Eric F. "Clement of Alexandria: a review of research, 1958-1982," *Second Century: A Journal of Early Christian Studies* 3/4 (1983): 219-244.
Pantuck, Allan J. "Solving the *Mysterion* of Morton Smith and the Secret Gospel of Mark," *Biblical Archaeology Review* Scholar's Study (October 14, 2009): www.bibarch.org/scholars-study/secret-mark-handwriting-response-pantuck.pdf.
—. "Response to Agamemnon Tselikas on Morton Smith and the Manuscripts from Cephalonia," *Biblical Archaeology Review* Scholar's Study (August 19, 2011): http://www.bib.arch.org/ scholars-study/ secret-mark-handwriting-response-pantuck-2.asp.
—. "A Question of Ability: What Did He Know and When Did He Know It? Further Excavations from the Morton Smith Archives," *Ancient Gospel or Modern Forgery? The Secret Gospel of Mark in Debate*, T. Burke (ed), 2013, Cascade Books.
Pantuck, Allan J. & Scott G. Brown. "Morton Smith as M. Madiotes: Stephen Carlson's Attribution of *Secret Mark* to a Bald Swindler, *Journal for the Study of the Historical Jesus* 6 (2008): 106-125.
Piovanelli, Pierluigi. "L'évangile secret de Marc trente ans après, entre potentialités exégétiques et difficultés techniques," *Revue Biblique* 114 (2007): 52-72, 237-254.
—. "Halfway between Sabbatai Tzevi and Aleister Crowley: Morton Smith's "Own Concept of What Jesus 'Must' Have Been," and, Once Again, the Questions of Evidence and Motive," *Ancient Gospel or Modern Forgery? The Secret Gospel of Mark in Debate*, T. Burke (ed), 2013, Cascade Books.

Pollard, Justin & Howard Reid. *The Rise and Fall of Alexandria: Birth-place of the Modern Mind*, 2006, Viking.
Porterfield, Amanda. *Healing in the History of Christianity*, 2005, Oxford University Press.
Preisendanz, Karl. *Papyri Graecae Magicae: Die Griechischen Zauberpapyri*, I & II, 2001 (reprint), K.G. Saur.
Quesnell, Quentin. "The Mar Saba Clementine: A Question of Evidence," *Catholic Biblical Quarterly* 37 (1975): 48-67.
Samain, P. "L'accusation de magie contre le Christ dans les évangiles," *Ephemerides Theologicae Lovanienses* 15 (1932): 449-490.
Schenke, Hans-Martin. "The Mystery of the Gospel of Mark," *Second Century: A Journal of Early Christian Studies* 4/2 (1984): 65-82.
Sellew, Philip. "Secret Mark and the History of Canonical Mark," *The Future of Early Christianity: Essays in Honor of Helmut Koester*, B.A. Pearson, et al. (eds), 1991, Fortress Press.
Smith, Edward R. *The Temple Sleep of the Rich Young Ruler*, 2011, SteinerBooks.
Smith, Jay E. "The Roots of a 'Libertine' Slogan in 1 Corinthians 6:18," *Journal of Theological Studies* 59 (2008): 63-95.
Smith, Kyle. "'Mixed with Inventions': Salt and Metaphor in Secret Mark," http://www-user.uni-bremen.de/~wie/Secret/SALT-PAPER.rtf.
Smith, Morton. *Clement of Alexandria and a Secret Gospel of Mark*, 1973, Harvard University Press.
—. *The Secret Gospel: The Discovery and Interpretation of the Secret Gospel According to Mark*, 1973, Harper-Collins.
—. "On the Authenticity of the Mar Saba Letter of Clement," *Catholic Biblical Quarterly* 38 (1976): 196-199.
—. *Jesus the Magician*, 1978, Harper San Francisco.
—. "Clement of Alexandria and Secret Mark: The Score at the End of the First Decade," *Harvard Theological Review* 75/4 (1982): 449-461.
Stroumsa, Guy G. "Comments on Charles Hedrick's Article: A Testimony," *Journal of Early Christian Studies* 11/2 (2003): 147-153.

—. *Morton Smith and Gershom Scholem, Correspondence 1945-1982*, 2008, Brill.

Trachtenberg, Joshua. *Jewish Magic and Superstition: A Study in Folk Religion*, 1939, Behrman's Jewish Book House.

Tselikas, Agamemnon. "Agamemnon Tselikas' Handwriting Analysis Report," *Biblical Archaeology Review* Scholar's Study. http://www.bibarch.org/scholars-study/secret-mark-handwriting-agamemnon.asp.

—. "Response to Allan J. Pantuck." Biblical Archaeology Review Scholar's Study. http://www.bib-arch.org/scholars-study/secret-mark-handwriting-response-tselikas.asp.

Van Hoye, Albert. "La fuite du jeune homme nu (Mc 14,51-52)," *Biblica* 52 (1971): 401-406.

Viklund, Roger. "Reclaiming Clement's Letter to Theodoros—An Examination of Carlson's Handwriting Analysis." http://www.jesusgran-skad.se/theodore.htm.

—. "Tremors, or Just an Optical Illusion? A Further Evaluation of Carlson's Handwriting Analysis," http://www.jesusgranskad.se/theodore2.htm.

Viklund, Roger & T.S. Paananen. "Distortion of the Scribal Hand in the Images of Clement's Letter to Theodore," *Vigiliae Christianae* 67 (2013): 235-247.

Watson, Francis. "Beyond Suspicion: On the Authorship of the Mar Saba Letter and Secret Gospel of Mark," *Journal of Theological Studies* 61 (2010): 128-170.

Also by Robert Conner

Magic in Christianity: From Jesus to the Gnostics
ISBN: 978-1-906958-61-9, 486pp/£14.99/$28

Available in bookshops, online or post-free direct from www.mandrake.uk.net

In 1906, theologian Albert Schweitzer wrote The Quest of the Historical Jesus. The book initiated the modern search for the Jesus of history and would prove to be one of the most important works on Christianity written in the 20th century.

Scholars steadily accumulated evidence for magical practices in the New Testament—and by the 1970s, books setting out the evidence were published.

Academic interest in magic in the Greco-Roman world increased dramatically—with the result that further connections between Christian and Pagan magic were documented.

It is a world that swarmed with prophets and exorcists, and holy men and healers who invoked angels and demons, gods and ghosts. Where believers practiced ecstatic spirit possession, struck others dead on the spot by pronouncing curses, used articles of clothing and parts of corpses to perform magical healing and exorcism, invoked ghosts and angels for protection—these practices are explained in detail by early Christian writers, and preserved by Christian amulets.

www.ingramcontent.com/pod-product-compliance
Lightning Source LLC
Chambersburg PA
CBHW071435160426
43195CB00013B/1908